Remember My Name

Remember My Name

The Authorised Biography of
Stephen Hendry

JOHN DOCHERTY

PELHAM BOOKS

PELHAM BOOKS

Published by the Penguin Group
27 Wrights Lane, London W8 5TZ, England
Viking Penguin, a division of Penguin Books USA Inc
375 Hudson Street, New York, NY 10014, USA
Penguin Books Australia Ltd, Ringwood, Victoria, Australia
Penguin Books Canada Ltd, 2801 John Street, Markham, Ontario, Canada, L3R 1B4
Penguin Books (NZ) Ltd, 182–190 Wairau Road, Auckland 10, New Zealand

Penguin Books Ltd, Registered Offices: Harmondsworth, Middlesex, England

First Published 1990
1 3 5 7 9 10 8 6 4 2

Copyright © Stephen Hendry Snooker Ltd 1990

Photographic Acknowledgements
The authors and publishers are grateful to the following for permission to
reproduce copyright photographs: David Muscroft pages 2, 34, 39, 41, 66,
70/71, 78, 120, 138; Randolph Caughie pages 6/7; Eric Whitehead page 22;
The Daily Record pages 30, 36, 37, 48, 123, 127, 139; Steven Pendrill, *Ayr
Free Press* page 46; John McAviney page 52; Terry Smith pages 56, 58, 74,
86, 111; *Daily Mirror* pages 78, 105, 117, 144; Frank Fennel page 106/107.

Every effort has been made to trace copyright owners but if there have been
any omissions in this respect we apologise and will be pleased to make
appropriate acknowledgement in any further editions.

Typeset in 12/14pt Linotron Bauer Bodoni by Goodfellow & Egan
Phototypesetting Limited, Cambridge.
Colour and mono reproduction by Anglia Graphics, Bedford.
Printed and bound by Clays Ltd, St Ives plc.

A CIP catalogue record for this book is available from the British Library.

ISBN 0 7207 1884 8

'To all my family and friends
and to all those whom I may not have
thanked enough along the way.'

Stephen Hendry

'I would like to thank Bostik, my major sponsor, for the financial support they have given me for this book, thus enabling the published price to be kept below ten pounds.

Bostik have been manufacturing adhesives and sealants since Queen Victoria's time, so I was delighted when they asked for my help in their advertising and promotional campaigns. It was quite an honour to be associated with a brand with such a great history and I was amazed to learn how diverse their business was in furthering major industries such as footwear, aerospace, double glazing and the consumer market.

Our association has now spanned several years and I have been involved in many activities with them such as TV commercials, personal appearances, wearing their logo and their latest venture: the sick seal appeal. Bostik are aiming to build a much needed hospital for sick and injured seals around the UK coast, something very close to my heart since there is a large seal population around my native Scottish coastline.

Bostik is certainly a brand with a great history and I am sure an even greater future. I look forward to working with them for many years to come.'

Stephen Hendry

Contents

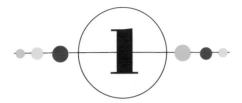

The Prince Becomes King

Sunday night in Sheffield, April 29, 1990. The city streets were virtually deserted. The only place where there was action was at snooker's Theatre of Dreams, the Crucible. There, amidst emotional scenes, a fresh-faced 21 year old called Stephen Hendry was rewriting sporting history. It is a memory I will take to my grave: the youngster from Scotland proudly raised aloft the coveted Embassy World Championship snooker trophy, after a superbly executed 18–12 victory over a gallant but outgunned Jimmy White. It was the stuff that dreams are made of.

After a gruelling 17-day marathon over the toughest, bloodiest course in snooker, the kid who wanted to become king had finally achieved his life-long ambition. It was hardly surprising that the small army of Scots fans, family and friends went wild with delight, raising the roof of the Crucible. Flash-bulbs popped, people wept. Some of the tears may have been shed for snooker hero White, who for the second time was experiencing the bitter taste of an Embassy final defeat following his 18–16 knock-down by Steve Davis in 1984.

Opposite: Aged 17, his first World Championship at the Crucible, 1986

Strangely enough the coolest character in the famous arena, which has witnessed so much drama over the years, was Hendry. There were no tears from him, but his eyes shone with happiness as he shredded the record books to become the youngest World Champion in the history of the game.

The previous youngest World Champion had been Alex Higgins, who won in 1972 when he was just 22 years and 11 months old. Higgins' long-standing record is now gone, and it's highly debatable whether another youngster will emerge to grab Hendry's piece of sporting folklore.

For Hendry is a one-off. He is in that special mould of sportsman who emerges, perhaps only every twenty years or so. He is like a Maradona of snooker. He is the new world number one who finally managed to break the Davis stranglehold on snooker which had spanned a golden decade. Hendry is up there at the top . . . and he's destined to be there for some time.

'This is everything I've worked for,' he told me, £120,000 richer (although big bucks have never been a driving force for the youngster from South Queensferry in Scotland). 'I always knew I could do it. Now I have, and it's a fantastic feeling.'

While Hendry was greeted by kisses and hugs by his mum Irene, dad Gordon, and girlfriend Mandy, manager Ian Doyle struggled to find the right words.

'I'm choked,' he said. 'I feel numb, and a huge sense of relief that Stephen has won the game's greatest prize.'

It was little wonder that Doyle looked dazed. Hendry's chief motivator and close friend had gone through an emotional minefield – and a few cartons of cigarettes – over the 17 action-packed, occasionally traumatic days in the snooker mecca that is the Crucible.

'This, in terms of snooker, is the greatest day of

my life. And there is no worthier World Champion than Stephen, who has worked like hell to make his dream come true. I have never been one for crying, or for showing a lot of emotion, but I must admit I was stunned by Stephen's victory. I was in a state of shock and didn't really know what to say to him. But I think he just had to look at my face to see how proud I was of him. I could not tell you the pleasure it gave me when the trophy was handed over to him. It's something I will never forget.'

There's no doubt that Hendry was a popular Champion.

But there was also a huge wave of sympathy for that lovable rascal, White, who disposed of the mighty Davis in the semi-finals, only to be trampled underfoot by Hendry. Said Hendry, 'I did not feel sorry for Jimmy, even though he has always been my hero. I have too much respect for him for that. He's a great player and it was a huge thrill for me to be playing against him in the final of the World Championship.

'I remember watching him once against Davis in the 1984 final, praying that he would beat Davis. And it was something else to be meeting Jimmy in the 1990 final. It was a tremendous match, and I know we will have many more great games in the years to come. Unfortunately there is always a loser, and on this occasion it was Jimmy. It can be a cruel game.'

The 1990 campaign, which was to unfold so gloriously, was Hendry's fifth at the Crucible, which has become a second home for the legendary Davis. In 1986, Hendry scrambled through the qualifiers, beating fellow Scot Bert Demarco, Paddy Browne, Wayne Jones and Dene O'Kane. That, in itself, had the snooker world buzzing about the skinny kid from north of the border who showed no fear of anyone.

13

Hendry's bold quest, however, ended in the first round during the televised stages, when he went down 10–8 in an epic against the formidable break builder, Willie Thorne. Thorne showed what a gentleman he is when he arrived at Hendry's hotel later that night and shook his hand for what had been a tremendous match. 'Stephen gave me the fright of my life,' Thorne said.

The following year Hendry got his revenge when he toppled Thorne 10–7, again in a first round confrontation. Hendry then made it to the last eight before going down 13–12 to defending champion Joe Johnson, who was then beaten by Davis in the final.

By this time, Hendry was fast becoming a big name on the circuit, an unrelenting potting machine who was getting stronger all the time. In 1988 he ousted Dean Reynolds in the first round but, in the next, was sent spinning to a high-voltage 13–12 defeat – by that man White. Then, of course, came last year's breathtaking Crucible run, as Hendry threatened to go all the way, before failing at the semi-final hurdle to Davis.

This year there was no heartache, only joy for this remarkable young talent. Even before a ball was struck, bookmakers Coral were offering just 2:1 against a Davis v Hendry final. Both men dominated the betting across the country, with White third favourite to end his hoodoo at the Crucible. The bookies almost got it right . . . almost . . .

Hendry, who has been encouraged – and occasionally bullied – throughout the past few years by CueMasters' road manager John Carroll, checked into Sheffield's exceptionally pleasant Hotel St George several days before the start of the Championship on April 13.

'I wanted to get as much practice under my belt as possible,' said Stephen, who carried with him the hopes of almost every snooker fan in Scotland. The St George is perfect. It's tucked away from Sheffield's busy city centre, has beautiful grounds and even a small pond if you fancy a spot of fishing.

When Hendry arrived with Carroll, however, the only thing he was angling for was that world title.

'The Championship was in my mind a lot, and I knew that Davis was the man everyone had to beat. He has monopolised the game for so long and he was heading to Sheffield knowing he had won the world title no fewer than six times, and was aiming for his seventh. With that fabulous record, Davis was the king pin, and rightly so, but I also felt that Jimmy White would enjoy a long Championship. And, of course, it would have been daft to write off all the other challengers in the tournament.'

D-Day for Hendry – joined by fellow CueMasters' stars Joe Johnson, Mike Hallett, Darren Morgan and Gary Wilkinson – was April 17. Standing between Hendry and a place in the second round of the £620,000 Championship was Canadian Alain Robidoux, one of the most feared and respected players in the game. Hendry predicted before the match that it would be far from easy.

'Robidoux is an exceptionally hard competitor who always makes life for his opponent as difficult as possible. I could not have asked for a tougher draw.'

What Hendry did not know was that controversy would erupt at the end of his 10–7 match which ended the following evening.

Hendry's pre-match forecast proved spot-on. For Robidoux, the best player to come out of Canada since Cliff Thorburn, gave as good as he got. And with the game balanced on a knife-edge at 7–7, Hendry's Crucible quest looked in danger of ending in disaster. But then luck – or whatever you like to call it – played its part in Hendry squeezing his way

into the last 16. In the 15th frame, referee John Street called Robidoux for a push shot, just after he had split up the pack and appeared to be in a frame-winning position. That gave Hendry the advantage he needed, and he stepped in to take that crucial frame and the next two, to leave Robidoux a shattered figure.

Afterwards, at the press conference, Robidoux, one of the nicest guys on the circuit, said he would be making no official protest against Street's highly controversial decision. But he did say, 'I did not think I made a push shot. I am a fair player and if I had made a push shot I would have called it.'

The incident certainly wrecked whatever Robidoux could do to produce a stunning upset. He admitted, 'I just could not get it out of my mind.'

Hendry, who was just happy to get through what had been an absorbing contest, commented, 'I did not see what had happened. At the time I had my head in my hands. But when I did get back to the table after John Street had called a push shot, it was my job to finish the frame off. Thankfully the next two followed suit.'

Sadly, at the start of the Championship there was much worse controversy involving the man of many moods, Alex Higgins. Higgins, World Champion in 1972 and 1982, unleashed all his infamous fury against snooker's top brass after being bundled out 10–5 in a first round shocker against Steve James. Higgins, under the influence of the demon drink, also shamed himself by punching press officer Colin Randal on his way to the after-match press conference.

'It's all very sad,' was Hendry's comment as he steeled himself for a last 16 meeting with Tony Meo. Meo played some good snooker but still finished up buried 13–7 by Hendry, whose confidence was growing as the tournament progressed.

Meanwhile, Hendry's CueMasters' stablemate Darren Morgan, the former World Amateur Champion from the village of Cwmfelinfach in Wales, was also making big strides. In the first round he defeated CueMasters' pal Joe Johnson 10–8 and followed that up with an impressive 13–8 second round win over another CueMasters' ace, Mike Hallett. That double act earned Morgan a quarter-final showdown with the biggest name in the CueMasters' camp, Hendry.

Morgan is a likeable man, and seems destined to enjoy a bright future in snooker. But perhaps the occasion was just too daunting, for the young Welsh wizard finally ran out of magic as Hendry sent him tumbling out 13–6. Hendry booked a semi-final clash with Merseyside star John Parrott, who had earlier upset him in the final of the European Open in Lyon.

'We have had many important matches and this one was no different,' said Hendry. 'But I was determined that 1990 was going to be my year.'

Parrott, meanwhile, had every reason to be quietly confident about his chances. After all he had reached the final the previous year, only to be blown away 18–3 by Davis.

In the early stages of their 35-frame battle, Hendry found himself in serious trouble. Parrott, in a mean mood, rattled in breaks of 60, 76 and 56 to move into a 4–0 lead. Then breaks of 38 and 70 helped Hendry to cut the deficit to 4–2, only to leave the arena that night 5–3 behind.

While his sleep that night might have been troubled, Hendry showed no sign of it the following afternoon. This time it was a different player on show as he rifled in breaks of 90, 63, 39, 51, 31, 55 and 36 to take five frames on the trot, and sweep into a 9–5 lead over a battered Parrott.

The next morning, Friday, April 27, it was Parrott's turn to tighten the screw in a match which was to see-saw all the way to its dramatic end. From being three frames down, Parrott, a former player in the CueMasters' camp, wrapped up six frames without reply to edge into an astonishing 11–9 lead. Hendry, however, is never more lethal than when his back is up against the wall. He displayed all his renowned character, conjuring up breaks of 70 and 64 to level the game at 11–11.

That proved to be the end of Parrott's latest Sheffield snooker adventure. In the final evening session, with everyone believing they were in for a match which would stretch to the full 35 frames, Hendry seized the 23rd frame thanks to a fine 84 clearance. It was the end for the brave Parrott as Hendry won the next three frames, and the last frame with a 74 break, to finish a very relieved 16–11 winner – with a fairytale final against Jimmy White burning brightly on the horizon.

'The Whirlwind' would be no push-over. No one needed to remind Hendry of that. Before cutting down Davis in the semis, White had taken care of Danny Fowler (10–4), John Virgo (13–6), and Terry Griffiths (13–5).

It was against 'The Nuggett' that White usually really sparkled. Yet White's prospects did not look too promising as Davis surged into an early 5–2 lead. Davis then went on to lead 8–6, but was caught cold with White grabbing seven of the next eight frames to turn the semi-final around to go ahead 13–9. While Davis hit back with all the skill and courage he is renowned for, White held on grimly for a brilliant 16–14 triumph, becoming only the fifth player to defeat Davis at the Crucible.

On Saturday, April 28, the Crucible was poised for the snooker fight of the century – Hendry versus the pale-faced, maverick White – with the snooker world knowing that it was about to witness a new name on the Champion's trophy. Sheffield was bursting with speculation.

The locals seemed to fancy White. Everyone loved him, and he was Matchroom boss Barry Hearn's last remaining hope in what had been an electrifying tournament. White was all psyched up for what he was hoping would be the greatest moment ever in his career, which has always promised so much but has not yet delivered the success of which he is capable. But the men in the know, the bookies, made Hendry a firm favourite to dent White's dream and take the silverware back to Scotland – the first Scot to do so since Walter Donaldson in1950.

Len Ganley, the genial giant of the circuit, had the honour of refereeing the final which would earn the Champion a place in snooker's Hall of Fame. Everyone expected a classic – a potting war – and no one left disappointed.

White, who had worked like hell for the tournament, drew first blood, winning the opening frame with a 42 break. Then Hendry raced away with the next, 73–13, courtesy of an immaculate 72 break in just eight minutes.

A 46 saw White win the third frame to go 2–1 up, astonishingly the last time in their 35-frame shoot-out that he was in front. A 32 break in the fourth levelled the match for Hendry at 2–2, and he went on to edge ahead 4–3 at the end of their opening session.

The second session that evening proved critical for both players. Hendry took the eighth frame with a 47 clearance, winning it comfortably 87–25, but then watched White turn on the style, winning the ninth 75–64 following a superb 67 clearance. That undoubtedly raised White's spirits and he pinched the tenth frame 68–57 to level the match at 5–5.

Hendry, however, refused point blank to buckle

as the tension intensified among the 980-strong audience who had been lucky enough to buy a ticket – plus the millions of viewers who were glued to their television sets.

Hendry punched in breaks of 42 and 65 to move into a 7–5 lead. But the gritty White bounced back, hitting a 62 clearance to steal the 13th frame 63–52 after Hendry had scored a 45. Neither player was giving an inch, although breaks of 53 and 108 helped Hendry stretch his precarious advantage again to 9–7.

Into Sunday and everything to play for. Manager Doyle, puffing away non-stop in a bid to calm his nerves, was jumping about like a cat on a hot tin roof. During the Championship he mostly sat in the press monitor room with Steve Davis's dad, Bill, who had a Havana cigar dangling constantly from his mouth. (When he is excited Doyle rubs the palms of his hands together. You half expect sparks to fly when he is around, and they often do!)

The only person who did not appear nervous was cool hand Hendry. On that fateful Sunday afternoon, he came out with his guns blazing. In an astonishing spell which reduced White to the role of spectator, the youngster, who only celebrated his 21st birthday on January 13, wrapped up four frames in succession to move into a 13–7 lead.

It was a joy to watch. Hendry was banging in breaks of 34, 66; a 104 clearance followed by breaks of 58 and 81 left the stricken White in all sorts of trouble. White managed to claw his way back into contention to trail 14–10 at the end of that third session. Hendry, however, was within sight of the pot of gold at the end of the rainbow, and was not to be denied. He took the 25th frame, ramming in breaks of 57 and 40 only to watch a valiant White peg the score back to 15–11, thanks to a 40 break followed by an 87 clearance.

The 27th frame, however, proved a killer for The Whirlwind. For Hendry, who must have nerves of Sheffield steel, somehow kept his cool, firing in a 108 clearance, the highest of the final. He then moved further ahead, 17–12, and wrapped up a spellbinding night's work with a 71 in the final frame of this classic snooker battle. If Hendry had wanted to choose a victory theme tune at that moment it would have surely been the '18–12' Overture.

White was gallant in defeat, but Jimmy is always sporting. 'Stephen played exceptional snooker out there,' he said. 'He potted some great long balls and his safety was impeccable. When I tried to play safe, the ball wasn't as close to the baulk cushion as I would have liked. Any half chance Stephen had, he would punish me.'

For White, there was the consolation of a runner-up cheque for £72,000. But that was small reward for a player who had put his soul into what might have been his last chance to become the World Champion.

Later, Hendry headed to the Grosvenor House Hotel with his girlfriend, Mandy, for the traditional winner's reception. Most of the Hendry clan were there, including his mum and dad, his young brother Keith and other close members of the family.

It was a star-studded night. Enjoying the celebrations were people such as Lee Doyle, Ian's 22-year-old son, who has ventured into snooker's management business with up and coming Scots star Drew Henry; former Rangers footballer, Kevin Drinkell; and Mick Hucknall, lead singer with the pop group 'Simply Red'. It was that kind of night – and it belonged to Stephen Hendry.

For Hendry it was the sweetest of moments – while the vanquished White could only look back on what might have been. Afterwards, the victorious Hendry party headed back to the Hotel St George to sleep on what had been a Championship to remember for a long, long time.

Stephen with Mick Hucknall of 'Simply Red' at World Championship celebration party, April 1990

2

The Christmas Present Stephen Will Never Forget

'Stephen had only one thing on his mind – and that was playing snooker.'

Irene Hendry was remembering how it all started. 'Stephen got his first snooker table when he was twelve. It was for Christmas, and just two weeks before his 13th birthday. At the time we were staying at my sister's house in Dalgety Bay, Fife. She was in Canada, so we stayed in her house before we bought our own.'

The present was a last-minute decision that was to change all their lives, for Stephen had never played snooker until his parents bought him that table.

'We couldn't think what to get him,' said Irene. 'I was shopping in Dunfermline at the time and saw the table in John Menzies. It cost £137. It was six feet by four feet, and looked smashing, so I went home to Gordon and discussed it with him. He had most other things a boy of his age would want – golf clubs, badminton racket, a football, so we decided to buy him the table.

'I'll always remember the expression on Stephen's face that Christmas morning. His eyes lit up, and we thought: "We've cracked it. He really likes it." And that was all that mattered to us.'

The twelve year old liked it, all right. Even now, his eyes widen as he recalls: 'The first time I picked up a snooker cue, I fell in love with the game.'

Aged 13, Stephen had been playing snooker for a year

The table that was to transform his life was put in his bedroom, squashed against a wall, which made some shots difficult. But the boy discovered he had a natural talent.

'I played on that table whenever I could. I would have a hit before I went to school, and I would play on it non-stop when I came home from school, stopping only to have dinner. Within two weeks I had scored a 50 break. I played my dad, and was beating him all the time. I was learning and loving it all, although I don't know if my dad felt the same.

'I wasn't tall then, less than five feet, and had to use the rest frequently. That turned out to be not such a bad thing, because the rest plays such an important part in any player's game. When I started on the professional circuit, I was five feet seven inches. I'm glad I sprang up in the years to follow, because it made playing snooker much easier.

Stephen collecting his first tournament trophy, the Pontins Star of the Future, aged 13 in 1982

'I realised I might have a future in snooker when I was just 13. Then, at the Classic Snooker Centre in Dunfermline, I hit my first century break. It was a marvellous moment. I was playing with my dad,

25

and after it I went through to tell the club owner. He said: "Were there any witnesses?" Clearly, he didn't believe me, and I don't blame him, for there were not too many 13 year olds banging in 100 breaks. I knew then that I could play the game.'

Stephen went down to Pontins in Wales, to play in the Under-16s 'Stars of the Future', to find out just how good he really was.

'It proved worthwhile, because I won the tournament. A lot of people were surprised, and I was over the moon. It was also my first money win – £100.

Stephen as a school boy

'From then on it was goodbye to school studies. I studied for four O levels at Inverkeithing High School, sat two, failed miserably, and got none. It wasn't that I was totally thick, but snooker took up all my spare time. The headmaster, Mr Mackenzie,

was very understanding, and allowed me time off to play in amateur tournaments all over Britain.

'Some of my teachers were a bit disappointed that I was not applying myself as well as I could, and that was understandable. To be honest, some of them thought I was off my head to think a daft wee

Stephen, extreme right front row, in his school football team

Stephen and his school class, middle row extreme left

boy from Scotland was good enough to make the grade in snooker. They must have thought they had a right day-dreamer, a kind of Walter Mitty. But, by that time, I had won a number of tournaments, some worth £500, which wasn't bad for a 15 year old.'

But for that Christmas present, Stephen might have wound up working in his dad's fruit shop. There's no doubt that the biggest early influence on his career was his parents. 'They let me do just what I wanted – play snooker – and my dad came everywhere with me. He never missed a match.'

But all the love and protection in the world could not save Stephen from the worst blow of his young life – the break-up of his parents' marriage. It was a blow he took very badly.

Stephen's second amateur win, The Scottish Amateur Championship, with his brother and his parents, in 1985

After so many happy years with Gordon, the split seemed inevitable to Irene.

'It was a gradual growing apart over a long, long time. We led separate lives, and it got to the stage when there was no meeting point. It's like falling in love . . . it's just as easy to fall out of love. I woke up one morning and knew that to break up was right, that the thing to do was to end our marriage. I don't wish Gordon any harm whatsoever. I wish him well, I hope he finds happiness, fulfilment and content- ment. Now if I'm watching Stephen in a tournament or exhibition match, Gordon is often there with his girlfriend Gillian. I am very pleased for them.

'Stephen took the break-up badly, but that's the difference between him and his brother Keith. Keith was aware of the atmosphere at home. Stephen, on the other hand, was wrapped up in his snooker, which was what we encouraged him to do so that he wasn't aware what was happening between Gordon and me. It was natural, therefore, that it came as more of a shock to him, and it still hurts both the boys. It can be difficult to talk about, but despite what has happened, Gordon will always, always, be their father. It doesn't matter that Gordon and I no longer love each other, that we don't live together. It's important that the boys talk about their father and don't try and avoid the issue.'

Stephen still has difficulty talking about the crash of his parents' world.

'I'll never forget the night my mum and dad told Keith and me that they were splitting up,' he said. 'I was 15 at the time, and it came as a horrible shock, for until it happened I honestly didn't know they weren't getting along. There were no raging argu- ments, at least not while I was in the house. But it must have been simmering away, until the whole thing reached boiling point. They were growing apart, but Keith and I knew nothing about it. Perhaps we were too young.

'That night, they sat us down in the living-room, and mum broke the news. It must have taken a lot for her to pluck up the courage to tell us. I couldn't believe it. I never thought such a thing would happen to our family. I thought that it happened to

29

other people. My immediate feeling was shock. Keith and I were just heartbroken.

'That's all history now. They have gone their separate ways. Dad is living in Musselburgh with his girlfriend Gillian. Mum and dad seem happy, and that's very important. I'm sure mum will find someone in the future. They don't hate one another. How could they after being married so long? And if they're at a tournament when I'm playing, they invariably talk to each other.'

A family photograph

Apart from the emotional upheaval, this was also a time when the champion-to-be did not have a pound in his pocket.

'When my mum and dad split up, my mum, Keith and I lived with gran in Kirkliston for about 4 months before moving into a council house. We were absolutely skint. Looking back, the house wasn't so bad, but it was cold. There wasn't much money coming in, as I had just started as a professional, and was earning buttons. It was left to my mum, who worked for the insurance services side of a banking corporation, to bring in the wage packet to look after us. We had to scrape for everything, but she did a tremendous job.

'The lean times taught me a lot. They also made me hungry! In a strange way, now it's like having monopoly money. It's weird. But it's brilliant knowing that if I walk down a high street, and see a leather jacket for £500, I can walk in and pay for it there and then. Despite that, I don't throw money around, and I hope I will always keep a sense of value.

'After Kirkliston, the house in South Queensferry, although it's only a three-bedroomed semi, felt like a castle.'

Once in a While a Star is Born

The meeting that was to change Stephen Hendry's life took place in November 1983, at the Stirling snooker club of an intense, fast-talking businessman called Ian Doyle.

Doyle had kept an appreciative eye on the booming snooker scene but, initially, had no thoughts of going into management. Born in Carntyne, Glasgow, in 1940, he left school at 15, and trained as an accountant. Swift promotion followed with a Glasgow building material merchant. But the young Doyle's sharp business brain led him to strike out on his own, in 1966, with his own ironmonger's business.

'I was always determined to work in my own right,' he says. 'The company I was with in Glasgow promised me directorships and all sorts of things, but even that didn't attract me. I really wanted to go out, put my own money on the line, and see what I could do.'

Snooker was a different ball game. 'I went into some of the halls in Glasgow, which were down-market basements, smoky, coin-in-the-slot operations.'

32

It was the amateur side that first attracted Doyle. 'I became involved initially in 1983 when some people approached me to see if I would sponsor any tournaments, including the Scottish Amateur Championship. I asked them what the champion-ship had been worth to the winner the year before, and they told me £20.

'It was ludicrous. I increased the money to £1,200, plus back-up costs and hospitality. We actually netted about £2,500 for the Scottish Amateur Billiards and Snooker Association — and Stephen won the Championship, aged 15!'

By that time, Ian Doyle had a good idea of what to expect from the young prodigy. Doyle and his long-time partner Jim Marley had just opened their snooker club in Stirling. It seemed like a big gamble, bearing in mind that there was already a club in the town. But Doyle and Marley had decided to go up-market, plunging £600,000 into an operation

Stephen's first Scottish Amateur trophy in 1984 aged 15 – the youngest ever winner

33

with 18 tables – now 25. However, on the winter's night when Stephen arrived with a young team from Edinburgh to play against the home side, Ian Doyle nearly missed seeing him.

Stephen and Ian Doyle at the Press Conference following the 1988 British Open final

'I'd seen him play in Junior Pot Black, but I hadn't paid an awful lot of attention to him then, although I thought he was a terrific player. I never even thought of managing him in any shape or form – and I wouldn't have seen him at all that night if it hadn't been for the luck of the draw. He was playing against my son Lee, who's the same age, so my wife Irene and I decided that we would just hold on and see that match.'

The then 14 year old, five feet, two inches tall Hendry made an impact that still has Ian Doyle shaking his head in amazement.

'I was absolutely staggered. I'll never forget it. He was so graceful, like a gazelle round the table. It was like seeing, if you can imagine, one of the top stars

34

in show business, like Frank Sinatra or Pavarotti. He was just shining there, absolutely shining. You could see the class written all over him.

'Lee broke off, and Stephen immediately producd a 49 break, a fair part of it using a rest. It was just the fluency, the sheer movement. And he already had an arrogance about him.'

Doyle wasn't the only one impressed. 'Coming home in the car that night, Lee said out of the blue: "I've just played the future World Champion tonight." I said, "I don't often agree with you, but you're right. That boy is going to be absolutely great."'

The first encounter with Stephen fuelled Doyle's growing interest in the sport. 'I became vice-president of the Scottish Amateur Billiards and Snooker Association, and we got a circuit organised worth £50–60,000 a year, running from August to May.

Being presented with the Scottish Amateur trophy by Archie Macpherson the TV presenter

35

'Seeing Stephen had a lot to do with me putting up the money for the Amateur Championship. Stephen beat Jim McNellan, one of the favourites, in the quarter-final, and came through to beat one of my club players, Dave Sneddon, in the final at the Anderston Centre in Glasgow. At that time Dave was probably the best amateur player Scotland had ever produced.

'Stephen led all the way to 8–6, and Dave pulled him back to 8–8. I'll never forget that final frame shoot-out. Stephen won it 82–0. He had just turned 15. It was great to watch him win against such an experienced player. There was no doubt that his bottle was absolutely fantastic.

Winning the Scottish Amateur trophy for the second successive year, aged 16

'Just a few weeks after that, there was the Forth Bridge Moat House tournament, with a lot of good players: Murdo Macleod, Eddie Sinclair, and pros up from England.

With Murdo Macleod on turning professional, aged 16

'In his first round match (the best of five frames), Stephen was 2–0 down, and 55–0 down in the third frame. He was playing against Brian Blues from Edinburgh, who was a Scottish international, and a tremendous player in his own right.

'Stephen knocked in a 67 clearance to win that frame, took the next two frames to win 3–2, and

37

went on to win the tournament. He beat Murdo Macleod, with Murdo giving him 14 start.

'I sat watching him after he had won, and it occurred to me that if the boy was directed properly, if he was managed properly, and if he behaved himself and kept himself on the straight and narrow, there was no way I could see him failing to get to the top.'

Stephen retained the amateur title the following year, 1985, beating Jim McNellan again at the Anderston Centre, after trailing 5–1.

'By that time, although I wasn't associated with the boy, I was so proud of him I remember saying to him at one of the intervals when he was 5–1 down: "You're too good to be in this position." He quietly turned round, and said, "But I've got him."

'It was weird. I laughed when I told other people there, then he came out in the evening, and won 9–6. It was unbelievable. That proved another point to me, that he had the lot – the natural talent, the bottle, the confidence and character.'

It was inevitable that the two would get together, and the call came in May 1985.

'I was still working on the amateur side, and I got a call from his dad, Gordon, to see if I was interested. I was living in Kirkintilloch, and had taken on Murdo Macleod at the time, but somewhere along the line it had dawned on me that I wanted to be involved with Stephen. I hadn't felt it was right or proper to approach Stephen, or his mother or father. When I got a call from Gordon, I went to see him and put an offer to them but I heard nothing more about it. I went back to Gordon, and he didn't seem terribly interested, which was surprising.

'The main aspect of the offer was to ensure that if the boy ever failed at snooker, he could come into my business. He would have a job available, and his future would be fairly secure. I guaranteed him a clothing allowance, and a steady wage of £250 a month, which was reasonable money for a young lad. But to be honest, there was no way I could see him failing in professional snooker, except if the direction was not right.'

Then Irene Hendry took a hand. 'She spoke to Gordon, and told him to phone me, basically because she was well aware that I was a fairly leading light in Scottish amateur snooker.

'So Gordon approached me again, and I said I was prepared to talk to him, but I wanted Stephen and his mum to be present.' The meeting took place in Stirling on a Friday night in September, 1985, and almost immediately Stephen signed up with Ian Doyle.

With Eric Park (holding cue), Promotions Manager of E. J. Riley – known to Stephen as 'Uncle Eric' – and Ian Doyle on the occasion of signing his first major contract

But the self-assured, trendy young star had yet to develop. 'At that time, off the table, Stephen was very introverted, a very shy boy until you really got to know him. I spotted a few dangers right away. He wasn't working properly at his game. The practice element was wrong, the general attitude was wrong, and up to the point when we signed contracts in October, he played three or four matches, and only won one. The results were terrible.

'At that time he was doing his practicing at Miller's in Broxburn with Robert Wemyss and Richard Miller, who both became very good friends of mine. They had done everything in their power to help Stephen, but they felt that he wasn't working properly and that it would be in his own interests for him to move.

'So I brought him to Stirling, and reorganised his working day, put him in a situation where he was not wandering into the club at one o'clock in the afternoon after being in bed all morning. He started putting in a full day's practice of up to eight hours, and initially he didn't like it very much.'

To break the monotony, Doyle arranged as many money matches as possible. 'There was the old story about Barry Hearn taking players down to the Matchroom to play Steve Davis, but I thought it would be much more advantageous to take Stephen out to meet various players throughout Scotland.

'We played for anything we could get our hands on; we played for £100, £50, £1,000. Bearing in mind that he had gone through a fairly rough patch in terms of money, he was hungry to win.'

The practice and the money matches paid off. In November, 1985, he beat Graham Miles 5–1 in the Mercantile Credit Classic in Warrington. 'That was a fabulous result because Miles was in the top 50 at the time. Then he beat Silvino Francisco to pick up his first ranking point. That was his best result to date. Neal Foulds beat him 5–4, but Neal was rising in the rankings at the time. So after weeks of work, Stephen could see what could be done.'

His big chance came in March, 1986, when he won the Scottish Professional Championship, beating Matt Gibson 10–5 in the final, which was televised.

'That brought him to the notice of most of the pundits, and through Eric Park, the promotions manager, we contracted to Riley's, the table and equipment manufacturer, the biggest name in snooker. That meant we could get a regular income for him, and set up his own company. We were fortunate to get a reasonably valuable contract. Its value depended on what Stephen was likely to do on the table, and was also based on his performances on the snooker circuit.

Celebrating a Riley sponsorship deal in 1986

'We signed the contract before his match with Willie Thorne at the Embassy World Championship in Sheffield in 1986. He lost 10–8, but his performance was memorable. It helped me in terms of communicating with him: that he was only going to get out of the game what he was prepared to put into it. It gave us both the lift we needed.'

Stephen Hendry, and Ian Doyle, were off and running.

4

Stephen in Disneyland

Overnight sensations are nothing new in snooker. So when the word trickled down from Scotland about a kid barely out of short trousers who was as good as Jimmy White, the smart money winked and smiled. At least until they saw him play.

Daily Express snooker writer John Hennessey is frank about it. 'I must be honest, I didn't see how he could be that good. But when I saw him at the Rothmans in 1986, I felt a mixture of excitement and fear because he was so good it was chilling.

'The first time I met Ian Doyle to do a feature on Hendry, I was smashed. I'd had a skinful, went down to the hospitality lounge and found Gordon Hendry and Stephen watching Jimmy play, so I plopped myself down next to Doyle, and told him I had a couple of slight problems. "I've not got a pen or paper, and I'm smashed."

'He said: "I'll be very interested in what appears."

'The next day, all I could remember was Doyle saying: "Every time I see that boy playing, it's like being in Disneyland", and that sent shivers down my spine. I was walking across to the railway station with my kid brother, and we were both nursing massive hangovers. He said to me: "That Scotch kid, he looks as if he should be delivering papers in the morning." I thought: "Oh, what a fabulous quote!"'"

Stephen had made just as dramatic an impression on veteran commentator Ted Lowe, much earlier. Lowe, the voice of snooker on television, whose first televised commentary was at Leicester Square Halls in 1954, remembers: 'Stephen's mum and dad brought him to me in Birmingham when he was about twelve. He was very proud, because it was the first time he had worn long trousers. They wanted me to have a look at him for Junior Pot Black, and he became the youngest-ever player on the programme. I said then that we were watching a future World Champion.

With McGuigan. From left, Stephen's dad Gordon, Diane Mulligan, Barry, and Paul Mulligan, CueMasters Irish agent

'He hasn't really changed in that time, and that has a lot to do with Ian Doyle. I give him full marks. The same qualities are there: coolness — he doesn't let anything upset him — whereas a lot of players are beaten psychologically. His fearlessness excites me, and he sees shots very quickly.

'One thing has changed, of course: his height. He's tall, which is an advantage for a player. When I first met him he was just a wee lad who had to stand on a box to see over the table.'

The almost childish looks and slight frame of the young Hendry confused almost everyone. Canadian star Kirk Stevens met him at the World Championship just after he turned professional in July, 1985.

'Stephen was with his dad, and I was with another player, who said, "This is a new pro". So I put my hand out to Stephen's dad, and said, "Congratulations, good to see you on the tour". Then out from behind Gordon comes this little kid. I almost died. I mean, it's scary to see this child, who's on a rough, tough tour. When Jimmy first turned pro, I'd seen him around for about four years, so he looked older, but Stephen looked even younger than he actually was. I looked at him, and I almost felt afraid for him, thinking of how hard the tour can be.'

Kirk recalls watching Stephen practising, but it was about a year before he thought, 'He's a bit useful. He hadn't got any results during the first year or so, because he was just feeling his way. Then I saw him playing Willie Thorne in the Embassy World Championship in 1986, and he looked like he was going to be an awesome player.

'What impressed me most was when I noticed he could beat guys who were playing well. He beat John Parrott, coming from behind to win 9–7, and he beat Dennis Taylor after being 4–0 behind.

'The most beautiful thing about him is that

there's so much of himself. He doesn't imitate anyone. Most kids tend to emulate their heroes, but he doesn't. He's not a clone of anyone.

An early professional exhibition match in Scotland with Dennis Taylor, 1986

'I didn't think he'd be able to handle the pace with Jimmy if it came to a potting game, but he did, and he made a believer out of me. Jimmy is the greatest talent in the game, but Stephen has more than Jimmy. He seems to have knowledge of when to tighten things up.

'Flaws? Everybody chokes sometimes; Davis, everybody. Sometimes you just miss. You've wound up wrong, and you haven't hit it right.'

Behind the scenes with John Parrott, 'the joker', in Scotland, 1986

Stevens scoffs at criticism of Hendry: that he can lack concentration, that he missed out on 'normal' life as a teenager. 'I think he's what every teenager in the world would like to be. He's doing what he loves, he signs autographs, he drives a nice car, he's got his house, and he's a very wealthy young man already.

'People talk about Davis along the same lines, you know. He sacrificed so much, but what the hell would he be doing otherwise? I know about being a teenager and sacrificing things. It's not a very pretty story.

'It's a beautiful thing that snooker has helped Stephen to grow up and develop his personality. Can you imagine Stephen Hendry, at 19, not being a good snooker player? He hasn't become big-headed, but if he ever does, he's got someone around to slap him down: Ian, his driver John Carroll, his mum and his dad.'

The match everyone wanted to see was the second round clash Stephen *v* Jimmy White in the 1988 Embassy World Championship. Jack Karnham, who is national coach and also runs a world-wide snooker foundation, has seen many matches. And he was in no doubt.

'I consider it to be the best match I've ever seen. Not in the sense that it was the most exciting game, but the total quality of the play was almost a slanging match at a supreme level. It wasn't just snooker, it was "I'm better than you"; "No, you're not". It was marvellous.'

Despite a result of 13–12 to White, Hendry proved he was a winner. 'When he was down, in the penultimate frame, he came out and played like a winner,' said Karnham. 'And remember the difference in age, 25 to 19. One wonders what Stephen will be able to do by the time he's 25.

'Steve Davis came to me when he was 14 and a half, with his dad, Bill. Bill asked me to have a look at Steve, because he didn't think he could do much for him. Steve had exactly the same qualities as Stephen, something very difficult to define. When we played, Steve expected to beat me. He couldn't, of course, because he was a lad, and I was a lot younger then, and played very well. But he conveyed to me that he wanted to beat me, and Stephen was exactly the same.

'Taking Davis and Hendry at comparable ages, there's no question that Stephen shows greater talent, but there are imponderables. The one thing I'd like to see him do is tighten up his technique. This sport is like any other; when you're an artist you're vulnerable. You see shots that are in your power, and a lot of players would say: "I mustn't try that". But if you're an artist, you're liable to try the shots other players can't play.

'Look at Alex Higgins. If you're going to talk

47

about gifts, Alex was so outrageous, with tremendous powers. So why is it that he won only two Championships? The first one he nicked when all the other professionals were asleep. Then he didn't win another for a dozen years. I'll tell you what went wrong: discipline. In 60 years there's never been a Champion who won a world title on ability alone. You have to harness that ability.

An exhibition match with Steve Davis when Stephen was aged 14 and another young player, John Herbert

'Steve Davis is an exceptional player, but no one has come along yet who has given him the eyeball. Jimmy's promised a lot, but it will never happen. If Stephen had got through and met Steve, he would have had the best chance of anyone of winning.

'Steve is not the most talented player in the world by a mile, but his talent is that he's still hungry and wants to win. I think Stephen's like that, maybe not as talented as Jimmy, but Jimmy's not a winner. I'd love him to win, but when you are so artistic, they seldom go together. Jimmy's like a beautiful boxer without a knockout punch.' Karnham is adamant about one thing: snooker will become even more of a young man's game.

'The technique of every game improves, and in snooker they've brought in new balls which are lighter and which permit you to screw the ball with total ease. Because of that, the cushions aren't used anything like as much as they used to be. Previously only top-class players could screw the ball. Now anyone can do it.

'They rarely want to pot with side, and if they do, they have problems. They've taken some of the lovely skills of the game away. They've trimmed the nap of the cloth so it's not as difficult, and now the youngsters can pot like demons. It's becoming a question of central ball striking, good cueing, and good eyesight. Everything's in favour of youth.'

Coach Frank Callan says: 'The kids see a good shot on television. They go and practise it, and in no time at all they're doing the things they see the stars doing. I've coached a girl of nine. She could barely look over the table, and she had a break of 88.

'I saw Steve at 20. We played a lot, and talked a lot, but Stephen has progressed without that kind of advice at all. They'd have had to cut off his arm to stop him being World Champion.

'Watching Stephen is like music to me. I can understand people going overboard about classical music, because good snooker has the same effect on me.'

No one had a closer view of the Hendry-White epic than the referee, John Street.

'For pure potting ability, that match was out of this world, and you'll wait a very, very long time to see another one like that again. Both were out for a gunfight. I don't think they played a dozen safety shots between them during the whole of the match.

49

It was joy, but they kept me on my toes. I had to run about a bit. It was really the kind of match where there shouldn't have been a loser, and I think that type of match should not be over until one of them has two clear frames. But with those two, that could mean going on all night.'

'When I first set out in the professional ranks, I knew that many of the other pros thought I was going into it far too young,' said Hendry. 'I felt differently, because I knew deep down I had it in me to make an impact.

'Some of them thought I would be murdered in my first season, and that's exactly what happened. It didn't hurt my confidence too much, for I realised it was all part of the learning process, painful though it might be. But prior to turning pro, I had travelled up and down Britain for two years playing in a lot of pro–ams. That was hard graft, and undoubtedly toughened me up.

'My one regret about turning pro when I did was that I missed the World Amateur Championship. It took place one month later. I felt I was good enough to win it, but looking back I made the right decision. Mind you, it would have been nice to win that title. I would have followed in the footsteps of my idol Jimmy White, and my stablemate Darren Morgan, who are both members of the amateur Hall of Fame.

'It wasn't long afterwards that I received my first real lesson – and what a lesson – at the hand of the player I admire more than any other professional – Steve Davis.

'Steve has dominated snooker for the past decade. There is no one to touch him in his dedication and determination to achieve perfection. He has a psychological edge over other players, and that was never more the case than on our ill-fated Scottish tour of January 1987. He destroyed me 6–0.

'I went into the series brimming with confidence, and at the end I felt as if I had been put through a meat shredder. At the time I remember Alex Higgins saying: "The kid will be killed." Of course, Alex was right, as Steve used me as his personal doormat

The Davis/Hendry shoot-out on the 1987 Scottish Tour

51

from venue to venue. It was a cruel experience. The Press had given the tour loads of publicity, billing it as "The King versus The Young Pretender". Every venue was virtually sold out, but by the time I had reached the Eden Theatre in Inverness for the second last match I found myself 4–0 down.

'I had never expected to win the series, but I couldn't believe what was happening. I didn't believe for one moment that I would be humiliated in front of my home support. The whole tour was a horror show, but the hiding in Inverness, in particular, hurt like hell. Steve beat me 8–1. I played like a novice, and the fans went home wondering why there was so much fuss about Stephen Hendry. I heard one punter say: "The boy is rubbish. I could beat him."

Visiting Barry McGuigan in Ireland

'From Inverness we headed to the Magnum Centre in Irvine for the last match. By that stage I felt well and truly destroyed, and my heart was no longer in it. I entered the arena, which was packed on a Saturday night, went through the motions, lost 6–3, and went home to pick up the pieces.

'My initial feeling was that I had set my sights too high, that the challenge series had been a dreadful mistake. I was a featherweight, who had gone in with Mike Tyson and got what I deserved. It was my worst experience in snooker, a nightmare from start to finish. But you have to hand it to Steve Davis. He had me under the cosh from the start, and never let up until I was stone dead. Against a youngster like myself, many other players would have reduced the pressure and let me grab a couple of matches, especially to give the fans more value for money. But not The Nugget.

'And it has to be said that he was right. For I felt in later matches that I was a much stronger all-round player. So while Ian Doyle came in for stick for putting me in the lion's den, I have a lot to thank him for. The Press gave us both pelters, but looking back it was all worth it. Out of the Scottish series emerged a much tougher Stephen Hendry.

'With that sort of experience, you can always bounce back in snooker. And it wasn't long before I had my revenge on Davis. Most players are really scared of him. And until our meeting in the 1987 Rothmans Grand Prix in Reading, he scared me too. It was one hell of a match. Steve went into it knowing he had wiped the floor with me in nine previous encounters.

'But this time I beat him – 5–2 – and I knew I had broken a psychological barrier. Now I always look forward to playing Steve Davis.'

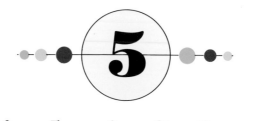

5

Sizzler in Sydney

On the way to his first major win, the 1987 Winfield Masters in Sydney, Australia

No one knows when the big breakthrough will come – the run of success that separates the super-stars from the merely good players. Stephen Hendry's golden season began at an unlikely venue, on the other side of the world. Ian Doyle had had a hunch about it . . .

'Stephen's mother, Irene, has played a big part in his success, in the way she brought him up in difficult circumstances. We are all very grateful to her, and just before the 1987–88 season, I pulled her aside and told her I thought this would be the year Stephen would win his first major. I don't like making these forecasts normally, but I wasn't just making noises. I was sure he was ready.'

So it proved. The season that was to shoot Stephen into the sport's elite was preceded by the best possible lift. In July 1987 he won the Winfield Australian Masters at the Royal Anzacs Club in Sydney. Admittedly, the field did not include Barry Hearn's powerful Matchroom team with Steve Davis and Jimmy White, but among the competitors were Cliff Thorburn, Alex Higgins, Joe Johnson and Tony Knowles.

Before the semi-finals of the 1987 Winfield Masters. From left, Mike Hallett, Stephen, Alex Higgins and Eddie Charlton

On his way to the title, Stephen beat Australian John Campbell, Thorburn and Higgins, before defeating stablemate Mike Hallett in the final — 371–226 over five frames. The prize was £21,800; his biggest yet. But more important than the cash was the confidence it gave him. 'It was a very creditable performance,' said Doyle. 'Just reward for the amount of effort, the slogging away at the practice table.'

After a brief holiday, Stephen returned to Stirling, his playing extremely impressive. 'He spent hour after hour just practising, which is the hardest part for any professional player,' said Doyle.

To play or not to play . . . Stephen recovering from an accident to his heels before the Lion Brown Masters in New Zealand, 1988. He went on to win, limping badly

Hendry started the new British season off with a semi-final place in the Fidelity Unit Trusts International at Trentham Gardens in Stoke-on-Trent.

Stephen's opening match against Neal Foulds was tough, but he came through to win 5–2. In the next, he faced another Englishman, Dave Gilbert, for a place in the quarter-finals. It looked a comfortable draw, and that's how it turned out, with Stephen cruising home 5–0. It was a similar story in the last eight, where he took the match against Joe O'Boye 5–2, without too many problems. He was brimming with confidence. Then the roof fell in.

The semi-final saw Stephen experience a humiliating defeat at the solid hands of Canadian Cliff Thorburn. The young Scot found out the hard way what a cruel game snooker can be. For handsome, moustachioed Thorburn simply brushed him aside, 9–1.

Stephen, not just beaten but demoralised, said wearily: 'It was like sitting in the dentist's chair, with Cliff doing all the drilling.' Later he reflected: 'That was the finest snooker exhibition I've ever confronted, or ever want to confront from an opponent. Cliff was a giant out there. He played out of his brains. His safety play would have delighted a Grand Master of Chess. Really, I never stood a chance, but looking back, I learned a lot just by watching him in action.'

Thorburn, ironically, failed to recapture the magic in the final, going down 12–5 to Steve Davis – who else? – who took the £40,000 first prize. The battered Hendry had £12,000 to console him for suffering his worst-ever tournament defeat.

'That defeat was a tremendous lesson for him,' said Doyle. 'While he had a great respect for Cliff, he never dreamt Cliff was capable of beating him 9–1. But Cliff played one of the finest matches I've

57

ever seen, that day. He was immense. It wasn't really a case of Stephen playing badly; Cliff's potting and safety play were out of this world. Absolutely fabulous, a tremendous performance from a tremendous professional.

'Nevertheless, it was four ranking points for Stephen, a very good start to the season, despite the one-sided scoreline.'

Goodbye Trentham Gardens. The roadshow moved on to the scene of the tournament that was to make the snooker world sit up and really take notice: the Hexagon Theatre in Reading, and the Rothmans Grand Prix.

First overseas trip. By the pool in Tokyo in 1987: Standing, from left: Steve Davis, Barry Hearn, Stephen; sitting, from left: Rex Williams, Willy Thorne, Tony Meo

Stephen, after the shattering defeat in Stoke, knew what he was up against. 'I realised it would be very difficult. You only had to look at the last three winners: Dennis Taylor, Steve Davis and Jimmy White. But I had set my sights on becoming the youngest ever winner of a major championship since Jimmy White won the Langs Scottish Masters in Glasgow in 1981, when he was 19.'

58

The championship started well. Stephen defeated Jimmy Chambers 5–1, which set him up for a last 16 meeting with Steve Davis. 'I hadn't beaten Steve in eight previous encounters, and I knew that not too many people gave me a chance. Ian and I had different ideas, although I knew I would have to change my game if I was going to crack The Nuggett. That meant mixing safety with attack, and it paid off handsomely.

'I got off to a cracking start, taking the first two frames, despite trailing 56–0 and 45–2. I knew then that an upset was on the cards, and went ahead to 4–1, although Steve pegged it back to 4–2 in the sixth.'

Instead of wilting under the pressure of a possible Davis comeback, young Hendry showed the stuff champions are made of. With his many fans in the auditorium roaring him on, he fired in a 72 break in the seventh, to romp home 5–2 – the best possible way to smash the Davis jinx.

Bolton Bomber Tony Knowles then stood between Stephen and a place in the semi-final. Again he sustained his brilliant run as he proved much too good for Knowles, winning 5–2 without really breaking sweat. Hendry was on the march, and in the mood to steamroller anyone in his path.

His semi-final opponent, however, was no mug: cool and collected John Parrott, the pride of Merseyside, and one of the most feared players around. It proved to be a gripping struggle, with Hendry emerging a worthy 9–7 victor. Just one step away from his first major, and Hendry was the talk of world snooker.

In the final his opponent was the hugely popular Irishman and former World Champion Dennis Taylor, whose scalps on his way to the Hexagon showdown included Bill Werbenuik, Cliff Wilson, Steve Newbury and Peter Francisco. Hendry was not to be denied. At just 18 years old, he trounced his vastly experienced rival 10–7, and earned his place in snooker's record books; plus a first prize of £60,000.

Ian Doyle was in no doubt. His youthful star had arrived. 'The most significant result was undoubtedly the win over Steve Davis,' he said. 'Despite earlier thrashings, I know that Stephen was supremely confident he could win. There was an air of determination about him.

'He showed tremendous grit and guts. Against John Parrott he trailed 5–1. He was 4–1 down against Dennis in the final. That was the greatest moment in my managerial career. I was so proud of him. At 18 years of age, what a marvellous achievement.'

The win put the season into an entirely different perspective. Two months earlier, Hendry was ranked 23. Now with ten ranking points from the first two tournaments, he was looking at going beyond the top 16. 'We both felt that a place in the top eight was not an impossible target,' said Doyle.

But obstacles, as well as opportunities, lay ahead. The Guild Hall in Preston was the setting for the Tennents UK, the second biggest tournament next to the Embassy World Championship. Despite Hendry's heroics in Reading, everyone knew Davis was still the man they all had to beat. Chasing his fourth successive UK title, he started red-hot favourite.

Equally, there was quiet confidence in the Hendry camp that, fired up by his Rothmans triumph, he could continue to dazzle at the Guild Hall. It was not to be. In the opening match, he was beaten, astonishingly, by Canadian Jim Wych, 9–7. True to form, Davis notched up a remarkable four-timer, coming through 16–14 in an epic struggle against Jimmy White.

At the after-match press conference, Stephen refused to make excuses. He said simply: 'Jim was the better player. He deserved to win.'

But it wasn't quite as simple as that. Ian Doyle explains: 'We were looking forward to the UK. It's a real test of skill and endurance. But two days before his match with Jim Wych, Stephen took ill. The day before the match, he spent most of the day in bed at the Crest Hotel. When he went over to the venue to practise, he still was not feeling well and he looked like death warmed up. The sensible thing would have been to pull him out, and it did cross my mind.

'Stephen, however, is a fighter. He was ill during the 1986 Rothmans and violently sick the whole morning before beating Robert Chaperon of Canada. I would have preferred him to pull out against Jim Wych, but he wouldn't hear of scratching from the Tennents. He felt he could go out there and win. He was 3–0 down, and went 4–3 ahead which was sheer guts. By evening, he was feeling really terrible, could do nothing right, and the end result was that 9–7 defeat.'

The Hendry camp took the set-back philosophically. As Doyle pointed out: 'Funnily enough, Stephen has never done well in the UK championship. In 1985 he was thrashed 9–2 by the Indian, O. Agrawal, a player he would expect to bury.

'The following year he also tumbled out, but there was no shame in that defeat – 9–8 to Alex Higgins. The match was a stormer. Stephen led all the way, and scored what looked like being a match-winning 55 break in the 17th and final frame. But because of lack of experience, he opened up an escape route for Alex, who stole the match with a brilliantly executed 82 clearance.'

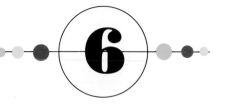

Hendry Plus Hallett

Brooding is a luxury no one can afford on the high-pressure snooker circuit, so Hendry shook off the depression of the Preston defeat, and headed for Northampton, and the Fosters World Doubles. In 1986, he and his partner, Mike Hallett, had done very well to reach the final, where they went down 12–3 to Steve Davis and Tony Meo.

This time their hopes were high for even more success in what was basically a fun tournament. 'The players enjoyed playing in it. It gave them the chance to relax,' said Stephen. 'The whole thing was laid back, because there was not the pressure of winning ranking points.'

In 1987, Stephen and Mike went one better. They won the tournament. 'Stephen was absolutely brilliant,' said Doyle. He hit Dennis Taylor and Cliff Thorburn with every weapon in his armoury. He reeled off break after break after break.

'But don't forget, it's right and proper that Mike gets his share of praise. He didn't pot particularly well in the final, but he played some tremendous safety, which caused Thorburn and Taylor all sorts of problems. That led to mistakes, and in would step Stephen to cash in. It was a great partnership which dovetailed perfectly. If Stephen was out of touch, Mike would grow in strength and *vice versa*.'

The Double H stable had not had an easy draw. The first match was against human beer keg Bill Werbenuik, Canada's genial giant; and a former dustman from England, Danny Fowler. Hendry and Hallett justified their star billing, coming through 5–2.

Their next match looked even more interesting: a tussle against the Irish pair, Alex Higgins and Eugene Hughes. But in fact they were swept aside, and again the score was 5–2. So to the quarter-finals, and the rock-steady partnership of Neal Foulds and Terry Griffiths stood in their path. Not for long: what could have been an uphill struggle proved to be a stroll for Hendry and Hallett, as they hammered the opposition 5–1.

With Mike Hallett and Steve Davis at the donor card appeal at Northampton General Hospital

63

There was no stopping Doyle's boys now. They simply shattered the South African uncle and nephew pairing of Silvino and Peter Francisco 9–4 to reach the final.

Thorburn and Taylor had been hugely impressive on their drive to the last match, underlining their brilliant form with a merciless 9–1 hiding of England's Steve James and David Roe. And they continued to sparkle as they raced into a commanding 5–0 lead, with Hendry and Hallett fighting for their lives.

But instead of collapsing in the heat, Hendry showed his mettle, and a devastating potting display saw him and Hallett forge into a 7–6 lead. After that, their opponents were merely whistling for time. Hendry and Hallett ran out 12–8 winners, to earn themselves a handsome pay cheque of £60,000, plus an additional £5,000 for the combined highest break of 182 (Hendry 116, Hallett 66).

Sadly, the World Professional Billiards and Snooker Association scrapped the tournament two months later because of disappointing attendances, and flagging interest from television. There was no doubt about it: the public wanted the head to head conflict of singles play. And there was plenty more of that to come, including a second major clash with Davis.

The Norbeck Castle Hotel in Blackpool was the next stop. The tournament, the Mercantile Credit Classic, had been won by Davis the previous year. Automatically seeded through to the fourth round, Hendry's first match saw him drawn against Joe Johnson, and he came back from a sluggish start, trailing 3–1, to win 5–3. Vanquished Joe commented: 'He's superb; an amazing young talent.'

So it was into the fifth round and a meeting with Silvino Francisco, on his day a dangerous and fearless potter. Francisco, however, couldn't compete with Hendry, and the youngster emerged a worthy 5–3 winner, to earn a quarter-final tilt against Steve Davis.

Could Henry topple the world's number one for a second time, after his success in the Rothmans? The answer was 'No'. In a match which could have swung either way, Davis's experience told as he won 5–3, before going on to defeat John Parrott 13–11 in a marvellous final.

For Stephen, at least it was another three ranking points. 'There was a great deal of talk about his explosive season,' said Doyle. But he was not yet in the magic top 16, officially, at any rate. And that kept him out of the Benson and Hedges Masters at Wembley. 'A great disappointment to the fans and the sponsors,' said Doyle, whose other player, Mike Hallett, was whitewashed 9–0 in the final by Steve Davis.

The turn of the year brought another upturn in Hendry's fortunes. He received a significant financial boost when Ian Doyle negotiated a new six-figure contract over five years with Riley, the snooker table manufacturers. But Stephen was much more interested in capturing his second major title. And that chance came in January, 1988, when the snooker circus moved into the Assembly Rooms, Derby, for the MIM Britannia Unit Trusts British Open.

Stephen's opening match against Terry Griffiths had all the hallmarks of a cat and mouse confrontation. The Scot, however, did all the pouncing, and won comfortably 5–1. His next match was against England's Tony Jones, and again Hendry came through with barely a scratch, 5–3. And that set up the quarter-final shoot-out everyone wanted to see: Stephen Hendry v Jimmy White.

'During the British Open, Stephen hit heights he had never reached before,' Ian Doyle remembers.

65

'The match against Jimmy was probably the finest nine-frame encounter ever seen on television. It was absolutely electrifying. The snooker was incredible. One minute Stephen would be on top; the next it was Jimmy's turn.

'The interval saw Stephen trailing 3–1, although there was not a lot between either player. Just before the restart, with things looking pretty black, I went down to see Stephen coming out of the practice room. He said to me: "Ian, I've just knocked in a 125 on the practice table."

Sharing a joke with Mike Hallett at the final of the 1988 British Open

'I snapped back at him: "What good is that? It's out there in the arena that you have to do the business." In some ways it was the right thing, in some ways it was the wrong thing to say to Stephen.

So I thought about it, and said: "Listen, son, I'm sorry. The fact is, Jimmy is brilliant, and is potting you off the table."

'The hatred in Stephen's eyes was quite unbelievable. His eyes were blazing. I looked at his face and all I could see was cold fury. Stephen's no big-head, but he hates being upstaged at the snooker table. I knew at that moment that he would come back and win. I told our driver John Carroll: "The game is in the bag. Jimmy is dead."

Exploiting the commercial possibilities of success. TV advert for Bostik super glue in 1989

'Now I did not say that out of lack of respect for Jimmy, because he is a fabulous player. But I did think back to a four-match challenge series between Stephen and Jimmy in Scotland the previous November. In each match, Jimmy got off to the better start, and each night Stephen wiped the floor with him. That was why I refused to write off Stephen at 3–1 down. I knew also that he was determined to make me eat my words. He went on to win 5–4.

'I love matches between these two boys. It's like watching World War III! They play a brand of snooker the public enjoys so much, knife-edge stuff. They can be brilliant, they can be erratic, but it's pure theatre.'

The stage was now set in the semi-final for a revenge match against Cliff Thorburn after that 9–1 drubbing in the Fidelity. Doyle had planned ahead for just such a clash. 'I pulled something of a master stroke when I realised Thorburn was in the same half of the draw in the MIM. So to try to soften the shock of the Fidelity defeat, I brought Cliff to Scotland to play Stephen for three or four nights.

'Stephen was very successful. He gave Cliff some of his own medicine. In fact, he beat him in every match, which was a boost for his morale. I knew it would be very difficult for Cliff to hit the heights of the Fidelity again. He felt Stephen would now be a really hot handful, and I felt that in that frame of mind, Cliff might fail to take one or two of the chances he had seized so successfully in the Fidelity, six months earlier.'

Doyle's game plan worked perfectly. In the afternoon session at Derby, Stephen stormed into a 5–2 lead. 'I will always remember Rex Williams, who was commentating on the match for ITV, say it was one of the finest sessions he had ever watched,' said Doyle. 'That was quite a tribute, because Rex has seen all the great matches. Certainly, the quality of snooker was tremendous.'

'Stephen was heading for the highest break prize, with 104. Then, in the sixth frame, Thorburn fired in a 112, and in the final frame of the afternoon, Stephen topped that again with a magnificent 118, which stood to the end and earned him an extra £6,000.

'Leading 5–2, Stephen looked in control, but he had to keep in mind that Thorburn was not known as The Grinder for nothing. The man has nerves of steel, and both of us were aware that Stephen had to be a little wary.'

This time, though, there was no great Thorburn fight-back. Stephen went out to the evening session looking ice-cool, and won the match 9–5.

For fans, the final proved to be an anti-climax, and something of a disaster for television. At the end of the first two sessions, Hendry led stablemate and good friend Mike Hallett 12–2. The following day, he needed just eleven more minutes to wrap up the deciding frame and win 13–2, and with it the £60,000 first prize.

Doyle commented: 'Stephen slaughtered Mike. It was merciless and frighteningly impressive at the same time. As stablemates, many people might have thought that Stephen would have eased up and perhaps given Mike the chance to make a match of it. Not a bit of it. As Stephen knows, the object of the exercise is to hammer your opponent. There is no room for sentiment. You go for the throat and don't let go.'

Doyle felt that Hallett, although playing well on his way to the final, had drained himself, and had nothing left by the time he got there. 'He just could not get going. From the first ball, Stephen imposed his will and authority on the game.'

The new champion agreed with his manager's assessment. 'I was surprised at how easy it was. And while Mike is a good friend, it was my job to drill him into the ground if I could. He would do the same to me given half a chance.'

Davis shows his concern as Stephen plans his next shot in the Embassy World Championship 1989. As it happened, Davis won

In a season becoming brighter with each tournament, the Hendry–Doyle partnership was on a roll. They headed back home, where Stephen was to defend his Scottish Professional title, a championship he had won for the two previous years. Once again, it proved a formality, with Stephen defeating Murdo Macleod 10–4 in the final to claim the £9,000 first prize.

Hendry's first round opponent in the dramatic World Championship of 1988 was Grimsby star Dean Reynolds. In a controversial encounter, Hendry came through 10–6 to set up a dream second round meeting with White.

Reynolds complained at the after-match press conference that Hendry had made a deliberate miss – although referee Len Ganley disagreed.

But it's a hallmark of Hendry's honesty that he expressed his 'surprise' over Ganley's decision not to call a miss. In any case, Hendry finished up a worthy winner – with millions of TV viewers delighted that the young Scot was about to pit his wits against White.

'Although I am World Champion now I will always remember my 1988 World Championship defeat by Jimmy White, when I went down 13–12, in what the experts call the greatest potting match ever.

'The Crucible was packed to capacity with everyone expecting fireworks from both players. Unfortunately for my supporters, the opening stages saw Jimmy hit me with everything. Before I knew it, The Whirlwind was in a 6–1 lead, and I was facing disaster. Just as quickly, however, I regained my composure, and wrapped up nine frames on the trot to lead Jimmy 10–6, and leave him on the ropes.

'I was cruising, and if Steve Davis had been in my shoes, he would have beaten Jimmy 13–6. Instead, I didn't capitalise on my big advantage. I lacked the killer instinct, and Jimmy, who played out of his skin, came back magnificently to sneak it 13–12. Jimmy was there for the taking, and I missed out. It was another important lesson: never give up in this game.

'It was a terrible disappointment. I was in tears, and so were most of my family. If I had beaten Jimmy, I'd have had a good chance for the world title, because I never thought that Steve Davis – who went on to beat Terry Griffiths in the final – was ever at his best.

'The match must go down on record as one of the all-time greats, an all-out potting war. And if I had to lose to anyone, I'm just glad it was against Jimmy. He has always been my hero.

'I first saw him play in an exhibition match in Dunfermline when I was 13, and I couldn't believe him. He did things with the white ball that I had never seen anyone do. He is unbelievable, a magician. With all his talent, it's baffling that the World Championship has eluded him for so long. Maybe it's because he's not as consistent as the other players, especially in the World Champion-ship where you have to sustain your form over a gruelling two weeks. I suppose my own lack of consistency was the reason why I have not done as well as I would have liked, although everything came together this year.

'My other idol when I started out was, of course, Alex Higgins, the player who did more to project snooker than anyone else. Without The Hurricane, snooker might still be languishing in the dark ages. I have played against him in practice, and Alex is absolutely tremendous, potting everything in sight.

'He is a genius, but he has become one of the game's great tragedies. Put him in a championship match now, and his concentration seems to go out of the window. Now, players who couldn't have lived with him in his heyday look forward to a match with him, because they think they are in for a fairly comfortable passage.

'Certainly Alex's wild life-style – particularly the ban he picked up for head-butting a tournament director in the UK Championship in Preston – hasn't helped. That kept him out of competition for too long, and his game suffered as a result. He became ring rusty, and since then he has struggled to find anything like his old form. I hope Alex comes back, but I'm afraid his glory days may be over.

'That forecast also applies, I'm afraid, to Kirk Stevens. He was number four in the world when I was starting. His match against Jimmy in the Benson and Hedges Masters in 1984, when he had a 147 and Jimmy had two centuries, is one of the best matches I've ever seen. I've still got it on video. I didn't know about Stevens' cocaine addiction until I read about it. It's a real tragedy. You'll never meet a nicer bloke.

The victor and the vanquished . . . with the Griff at the Regal Masters, 1989

'I can honestly say, hand on heart, that there is no player on the circuit whom I actually dislike. But in my first two seasons I hated competing against players who used a lot of safety – men like Cliff Thorburn, Dennis Taylor, Terry Griffiths, and Steve Davis. The reason was simple. They stifled my natural attacking flow, and I found it difficult responding because I didn't know how to play safety, and that really got my back up.

'Thankfully, that has changed now. I have learned that safety is a vital part of any player's game, and without it you're a dead duck. It's a bit like playing chess, and until I got the hang of it I was being destroyed.

'While I've said I never disliked any of the players, one thing did annoy me when I started out on the pro circuit. Some of the guys never showed me any respect. They clearly believed that I was just another promising kid, and the only way I was heading was down the way. That made me even more determined to make an impact.

'It's funny looking back, for when I started winning, they became a lot friendlier and talked to me a lot more. Instead of being an outcast, I was slowly becoming one of the lads. I suppose to earn that respect from the pros is one of the hardest things in snooker. Until you get to the top, no one gives you the respect you really deserve.'

7

Black October

Stephen Hendry went into the season of 1988–89 with great expectations. But his dreams of continuing a golden run were destined to plunge into a nightmare.

Stephen experienced one agony after another. His career so far had had a fairytale quality about it. Now he found out the hard way that the honeymoon was over. First came a temporary split with his girlfriend Mandy. Then came an anxious few weeks when his mother Irene went to hospital for an operation that was to keep her off work for three months. Worst of all was the black month of October 1988, when his one-time minder and close friend, Tommy McEwan, accused him of taking drugs to boost his sex life with Mandy.

Wonder boy Hendry became blunder boy, flopping dismally in the first two tournaments of the season, the Fidelity Unit Trusts International at Stoke-on-Trent, and the Rothmans Grand Prix at Reading. They were shocking times indeed for Stephen, who confessed: 'It was like a horror movie. Nothing went right. The whole world seemed to be piled on my shoulders.'

The bad spell hurt the young star deeply, although he always did his best to hide the mental scars. It also hurt Ian Doyle. 'It was far from being a vintage year, after all the fantastic memories of the previous season. So many things went wrong. Some people who didn't know any better said part of the reason for Stephen's collapse was that I pushed him too hard, that the work-load was proving too heavy a burden.

'It's absolute nonsense. Before the start of the season, Stephen had a ten-week holiday, which was extended to twelve weeks because he wanted to go on holiday to Portugal in the second week of August. He went with Mike Hallett, his mother Irene and his brother Keith.'

It was a break that was to prove costly. For during that time Stephen devoted himself almost entirely to his number two passion – golf. 'Every spare minute of the day he would play golf,' said Doyle. 'If it wasn't at Gleneagles, it was at Renfrew; if not at Renfrew then Erskine. If there was a golf course he had to play it, and his love of the game undoubtedly threatened his career.

'At the end of the holiday he was due back at the club to start serious practice for the start of the season. But he had made many good friends in the golfing world – Billy Marchbanks at Gleneagles and John Chillas at Stirling – and he continued to pursue his love affair with the game even when his holiday time was over.

'It was a disastrous move on his part. His practice time was effectively cut back to about two hours a day, instead of six or seven hours slogging it out at the table to get himself razor-sharp. Where he went wrong was thinking two hours were long enough.'

Incredibly, golf had become the top priority, and to make more time for it, Stephen began turning up at the snooker club early in the morning. Doyle continued: 'Some mornings he would shock me because he could be sitting in his car in the car park before the club had even opened. He would get on the table, hit some balls and zoom, he was off to play golf.

Above: Stephen's very first day on the golf course

Above right: Within a matter of months Stephen started looking the part

'There was no way I was going to haul him over the coals for not doing enough work. I did mention it on a couple of occasions, but he just smiled and said he was confident he was playing OK. So basically I left him to it. My view was that he was 19, he'd been a professional since the age of 16, he was one of the world's top players, and he'd reached the stage when he had to make decisions for himself.

'Then came the start of the season when so much was expected of him. He felt he was in the right groove, that he wasn't playing badly. But what he did not realise was that after his brilliant performances of the season before, Hendry the hunter had become every player's target. He was there to be shot at. Instead of having to build himself up to meet the top players, he found himself one of them, one of the game's elite.'

In the Fidelity, he confronted Steve James, a rookie who finished the previous season in a blaze of glory in the Embassy quarter-finals, when he performed magnificently before going down 13–12 against Cliff Thorburn. That result should have served as ample warning to Stephen. He should have realised that James was a formidable opponent, and that his confidence had received a huge boost when he came so close to taking Thorburn.

That was certainly Ian Doyle's view. But Stephen ignored the message. James wiped him off the table. 'Stephen's concentration was unbelievably bad, and his interest was non-existent. For all the interest he showed he could have gone out of the arena for a cup of tea and returned when it was his turn to play.'

Stephen agreed with his manager's brutal assessment. 'It was a rotten performance. Steve James is a good player and is improving fast. I should have beaten him. My head was in the clouds, I wasn't thinking properly, and Steve grabbed his chance and punished me badly. It was a terrible start to the season.'

From the gloom of Stoke, Hendry headed for London's Café Royal for a black-tie match against Terry Griffiths in the new London Masters, an invitation, non-ranking tournament. Stephen had no problems, winning 4–0, but it was not one of his best performances.

'Terry played the worst snooker I have ever seen him play,' said Doyle. 'He just couldn't pot a ball. If you had left a red on the edge of the pocket, and asked Terry to pot it from three feet, he would have been struggling. Stephen did what he had to do, without playing particularly well, and his confidence was flying high again.'

But there were more danger signals ahead. 'The next day we were in Blackpool for a match against a young newcomer, Steve Campbell. The match was a qualifier for the Canadian Masters, and the lad was so nervous I felt sorry for him. Stephen opened with a 99, then 112; it was brilliant. Just as quickly he went to pieces, and struggled to get through 5–2.'

Two wins in two nights. Stephen was back on song – or was he? The Rothmans Grand Prix, scene of his major triumph in 1987, was to provide the answer.

'I went to Reading with every intention of retaining the championship,' said Stephen. 'It meant an awful lot to me as it had been my first world-ranked success. But my hopes were to be shattered in a match that will haunt me for years.'

His first opponent was Ian Williamson from Leeds, a player, said Doyle, 'so slow that the seasons come and go when he's at the table. He is not the easiest guy on earth to play.'

The manager's fears were confirmed when he saw the score on teletext at his home in Bridge of Allan. 'Two–nothing for Williamson – I nearly fell off my chair. I immediately got on the phone to Stephen's driver, John Carroll, who was at the match, and gave him quite a bit of verbal. Of course my anger was not against John. It was directed at just one person, Stephen Hendry.

'Stephen picked himself up and came through 5–2. Obviously, he had listened to the comments I made via John. I knew Stephen's attitude at the time. He would be saying to himself: "I'm going through a sticky patch, and have got to wind myself up. I'm going through a rough spell, but I'll be OK."

'But although he won the match, I was worried, for I knew there was a question mark over his concentration, and had been right from the start of the season.'

Stephen, in fact, did have another reason for his lapse in concentration. On the day before the débâcle at the hands of Steve James in the Fidelity, he was told his mother, Irene, had to go into hospital. She underwent surgery two days before his second round match in the Rothmans. 'It was an upsetting time, a worrying time,' he said.

In the second round of the Rothmans, Stephen was drawn against Doug Mountjoy, a highly experienced player, but one reckoned to be in the twilight of a distinguished career. But it was his young opponent who wound up in the twilight.

'Everyone knew how hard Doug had been trying to get in shape for the new season,' said Doyle. 'He received coaching from one of the gurus of snooker, Frank Callan, and put in an enormous amount of practice in the summer months.'

What happened stunned the snooker world. Mountjoy took Hendry apart 5–1 after losing the opening frame. Said Stephen: 'To lose my title in such a manner was bitterly disappointing. I didn't go into the match expecting to cruise it; I expected it to be tough, for Doug is a seasoned campaigner. But it was a bad, bad defeat, and I knew Ian Doyle would be fuming.'

He was right. Manager and player had a heated face to face showdown. 'I pointed out how badly he was playing, how he was letting himself down, and to get back to basics,' said Doyle. 'I told him to get down to the hard graft, and lock himself away in a practice room for as long as it would take for him to get his act together again. Instead of playing on his own championship table in the Stirling club, he went into one of the private rooms where there could be absolutely no interruptions. That room became his very own prison for six hours a day.'

81

Said Stephen: 'It seemed like hell at times, a bit like solitary confinement. But the sheer monotony of it helped my game and my concentration, which has a tendency to go out of the window from time to time.

'Deep down, I knew that I was playing too much golf. The trouble is that I really love the game. I've cut my handicap to eleven in the past two years, and if I wasn't a snooker player, I'd like to have crack at becoming a golf professional. But snooker's my job, so I had to cut back on golf. I didn't much enjoy it, but it had to be done.'

It was a shaky Hendry who prepared for the opening round of the Canadian Masters in Ontario against Danny Fowler. 'The set-backs had dented his confidence,' said Doyle. 'He was under tremendous pressure. There was growing speculation on the circuit that the kid was struggling, that perhaps he had blown himself out. Stephen was very much on edge.'

But his courage was not in question, and he pulled through 5–2. 'I knew what was at stake, and I just wanted to get this first match out of the way. It was so tense out there, and I was very relieved to win. I knew I couldn't afford another early exit.'

Hendry's next opponent was wise-cracking Cliff Wilson, the Welsh wizard who is capable of producing so much magic when he's in form. Fortunately for the Scot, on that October day Wilson disappointed, and Hendry raced home a comfortable 5–1 winner.

The third round produced a potentially lethal challenge from the big home hope, Cliff Thorburn. It was a daunting test. But 24 hours before the match, Stephen faced another test – and there wasn't a snooker table in sight.

The front-page headline in an English newspaper screamed: 'Stephen Hendry in Love Drug Shock'.

Inside, the paper continued: 'Minder reveals the shocking sex and drugs secrets of snooker's golden boy and his blonde.' And 'Passion Potion Sent Steve Potty'.

Stephen and Ian Doyle were stunned as the lurid allegations were read to them in a transatlantic phone call. Stephen's ex-minder, Scot Tommy McEwan, was claiming to lift the lid off Stephen's and Mandy's 'amazing romps'. How 'Stephen Hendry went potty for sex after sniffing a powerful love potion'. That potion was said to be 'poppers', a liquid stimulant which acts as a sex booster.

'It is wild and completely untrue,' protested Doyle.

The sex-and-drugs allegations horrified Hendry and Doyle. But they were not surprised by the identity of the man claiming to spill the beans. Tommy McEwan had taken up the part-time job as minder/driver for Stephen at the start of the 1987–88 season. He was also to drive Mike Hallett, and, said Ian Doyle, did the job very well for a while. Then he and his wife split up.

At the British Open in Derby, in February 1988, Tommy was suspended. 'The reasons were quite simple,' said Doyle. 'He was always going out on the town, was a real disco bird, and was always on the hunt for women, which was banned on business trips.

'After the suspension, he came back on the road just before the World Championship in April. Then Stephen and Tommy had a bust-up, basically because Stephen knew what Tommy was up to and was unhappy about it. After all, it was Tommy's job to look after Stephen and Mike, and he was failing miserably.

'Despite the growing unhappiness over Tommy's many night owl flights, we got through the World Championship, although it was becoming clearer by

83

the minute that drastic action would have to be taken.

'Then we went into the new season and Tommy's general attitude and bad time-keeping made his position in the company virtually impossible. The end finally came when he failed to turn up at my house in Bridge of Allan one morning to take Mike to Glasgow Airport for a flight to Manchester, where he was playing an exhibition.

'It was the last straw, so I fired him. He was pretty shattered and asked me for one more chance, but I pointed out that he had finally blown it.'

But Doyle had not seen the last of Tommy McEwan. 'Two weeks later he turned up at the snooker club in Stirling, and said that as a result of his marriage break-up, his electrical business was in financial trouble, and he owed the bank £12,000. He was skint and desperate for cash.

'He asked me if I could help him out through this bad period. When he was told no, he threatened to sell some story about Stephen to one of the English tabloids. My immediate reaction was to tell him to go ahead. I wasn't particularly concerned. In my book, Stephen is a model professional, in the mould of Steve Davis.

'I told Tommy he had no story to sell, but I was surprised and disappointed by what he was saying, because he had idolised Stephen. I just couldn't see him dragging himself through the gutter by trying to blacken Stephen's name with some wild, completely untrue allegations. They had been good friends, and had played golf together. His grievance was not against Stephen, but against me, for giving him the bullet.

'I lost any respect I'd had for him. When he said he was going to the newspapers, any chance that I might have reconsidered his position was killed stone dead.'

Doyle continued: 'I have to say that all Tommy's problems were self-inflicted. He's a Peter Pan, never out of discos, which for a man in his middle thirties, and married with two kids, was a bad scene. Sometimes he enjoyed one drink too many, and he owed money to a number of people in Stirling.

'Because of all these problems, I can only assume that his mind was deranged. But I'm led to believe that he was paid around £20,000 for his sick sortie into journalism.

'One thing's for sure. He's still a member of Spencer's snooker club in Stirling; his membership has never been cancelled. But if he ever shows his face in the club, I will be very tempted to boot his backside.

'But he hasn't got the bottle to come anywhere near us. Too many people hate him for what he did. God knows how he can live with himself.'

Thanks to the unwelcome intervention of McEwan, Stephen faced the remainder of the Canadian Masters with his brain in turmoil. But he buckled down to the task of putting the events at home to the back of his mind, and prepared to face Cliff Thorburn.

Displaying tremendous character, he defeated Thorburn 5–4 to set himself up for a semi-final against Steve Davis, who had won the season's opening two world-ranked tournaments, the Fidelity and the Rothmans. But Hendry's victory did not delight Doyle. He said with brutal honesty: 'It was the worst performance I have seen from either player. Cliff could have won 5–0; Stephen could have won 5–0. It was a shame there had to be a winner.

'The whole thing was a comedy of errors, although neither player had anything to smile about. The feeling I got was that Cliff was frightened of Stephen. I don't mean to be unkind in

saying that. He had beaten Cliff in a handful of exhibitions, and thrashed him on the way to winning the British Open. I think he gave Stephen too much respect, and Stephen scraped through on the sudden-death black ball.'

That dramatic escape gave Hendry another tilt at The Nuggett, a match that was evenly poised right up to the twelfth frame, with Davis ahead 6–5. Hendry looked certain to level when he led 73–8 which left Davis needing four snookers. But a disastrous free ball situation saw Davis go on to pull off an amazing recovery and steal the frame 74–73. Davis rolled home 9–5.

Opposite: Stephen with his handsome dhow trophy

Receiving from John McKenzie, Managing Director Alloa Brewery Company Limited, the Scottish Skol Sports Personality of the Year award, 1989.

'That knocked the stuffing out of me,' said Stephen. 'I should have been shot for throwing away that frame. You never let Davis off the hook.'

Davis and White, those two great rivals, went on to compete in the final, White winning 9–4.

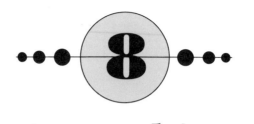

Ecstasy and Agony

November, 1988, was a crucial month for Hendry. His confidence bruised by early defeats in the Fidelity and the Rothmans, his reputation was on the line as he drove into Preston for the £400,000 Tennents UK Open. Outside his own camp, not too many people gave the youngster much of a chance. The tournament had never been a happy one for him.

His first attempt in 1985 had seen him thrashed 9–2 by the little-known O.B. Agrawal. But he did salvage something from the embarrassment the following year, when he reached round three before succumbing 9–8 in a memorable tussle with Alex Higgins. In 1987, he battled through to the third round again, but failed to find his best form, in a bitterly disappointing 9–7 defeat against Canadian Jim Wych.

So, as he prepared for his fourth crack at what was becoming a jinx event, the 19-year-old Hendry was up against it. The bookies certainly did not rate his prospects. One offered odds over him at 11–1, behind 5–4 favourite Steve Davis and 9–2 second favourite Jimmy White. If you fancied a punt on Doug Mountjoy, you could get anything between 200–1 and 250–1 . . .

When Stephen booked into Room 415 at Preston's Crest Hotel, his immediate ambition was simply to get past that tantalising third round for the first time. The critics were hovering in the wings waiting to see if he continued his lack-lustre run.

Said Hendry: 'I was under pressure all right, but that's something I thrive on. The championship, which had not been very kind to me in the past, was important for two reasons. I had to win back my confidence, and I had to avoid slipping down the world rankings.'

Stephen's opening match at the Guild Hall was against Irishman Tommy Murphy. The confrontation started at 2 pm on Saturday, November 12. By the end of the night, Hendry had shrugged off earlier set backs, winning easily enough, 9–4, without looking anywhere near his best. But it was the result he needed, and it sparked off a run of success that silenced the snipers who thought the pressure of being a teenage superstar was getting to him.

In the fourth round, four days later, he disposed of England's Colin Roscoe 9–3, showing flashes of his old magic. But the heavy brigade were on the horizon, starting with the formidable figure of Willie Thorne, one of the greatest break builders in the game. At stake was a place in the quarter-finals, with both players knowing that Cliff Thorburn and Steve Davis were in the same side of the draw.

That was all the incentive Hendry needed. Although still below his best form, he brushed Thorne aside 9–4. That guaranteed him a cheque for £12,000, and a meeting with his old adversary Thorburn, a tough opponent. Yet when Hendry left his hotel for the venue, just 400 yards away, his confidence was on a high. And it didn't take the

Canadian long to feel the lash of the Hendry whip.

Stephen swept into a 7–0 lead, and although Thorburn grabbed the next two frames, the Scot was not to be denied. He won the tenth frame with a clinical 69 break and seized the eleventh 88–12 to blitz his opponent 9–2. It was sweet revenge for that 9–1 spanking in the Fidelity 15 months earlier. But Thorburn was not convinced Hendry had hit the heights. He commented: 'I know he beat me 9–2, but there were three frames he fluked, and his rhythm was not there.'

Rhythm or not, there was no denying that it was an astonishing winning margin, and Hendry was happy enough. 'I had beaten Cliff in our two most recent meetings, and I felt I had it in me to complete the hat trick. But to be honest, I never expected 9–2. I knew then that my game was buzzing.'

Now, looming ahead in a tremendously testing draw, was the seemingly invincible figure of Steve Davis. For the past nine years, Preston had been The Nuggett's very own gold-mine. He had won the title in 1980 and 1981 with runaway victories over Alex Higgins (16–6) and Terry Griffiths (16–3).

Davis, who loves the atmosphere of the Guild Hall – and who could blame him – went on to complete a four-timer between 1984 and 1987. During this fabulous spell, no one escaped the Davis hammer. In 1984 he toppled Higgins in the final, 16–8. In 1985 he chopped down Willie Thorne 16–14, a desperately close affair which Thorne should have clinched, but for missing a match-winning blue into the centre pocket. In 1986 it was Neal Foulds' turn to come under the cosh, Davis streaking home 16–7. And Davis made it four in a row the following year, defeating Jimmy White 16–14 in an epic final. It was hardly surprising that Davis, unbeaten in a record 27 matches in the Tennents, started 3–1 on to halt the Hendry revival.

CueMasters accountant John Gilmour had promised to shave off his beard if Stephen won the Regal Masters in Scotland in 1989. It turned out to be a rash promise!

Hendry was not dismayed by the scale of the task in front of him. Nor was he frightened by remarks made by his stablemate John Parrott – clobbered earlier by Davis – that the man was 'a freak' and 'unbeatable', and that 'no one could touch him'. Stephen said calmly: 'I don't agree with John. Steve is the world number one, but he's human, and there to be beaten.'

Brave words, but Hendry knew it would take a Command Performance to smash the Londoner's monopoly in the event. It was, effectively, the longest-running show in snooker. No other player in modern times had ever gone 27 games unbeaten in any one championship. 'A fabulous record,' Hendry agreed, 'but even machines break down.'

Davis had had a turbo-powered start to the season, winning the opening tournaments, the Fidelity and the Rothmans, and finishing second to Jimmy White in the Canadian Masters. The bookies were in no doubt. At 1.30 pm on that Friday, November 25, with the Guild Hall filling up rapidly, they offered Hendry at 9–4, odds snapped up by a number of patriotic Scots enjoying refreshment in the adjoining bar.

Shortly after 2 pm, the players swept through the curtains into the auditorium, to be greeted by a tremendous roar from almost 2,000 spectators. Davis smiled, and delivered his usual polite bow to the audience. Hendry, his face a mask of secrecy, obviously had something on his mind. Davis was about to find out the hard way just what it was.

In the now-hushed auditorium, Hendry settled down quickly, scoring a 48 break which helped him take the opening frame 78–40. Just 17 minutes later he was 3–0 up. Playing with marvellous assurance, he won the second frame 111–0, with breaks of 33 and 78, and the third 115–0, with breaks of 49 and 66. Suddenly those bookies' odds looked crazy.

Hendry, mean and majestic, did not let up. He grabbed the fourth frame 77–38, thanks to a useful break of 35. One hour into the match, with the score an eye-rubbing 4–0, the players took a 15-minute break. When they returned, there was no hiding place for Davis.

Breaks of 51 and 37 saw Hendry take the fifth, 108–17. And he should have gone 6–0 up in the next, when he led 37–1, only to miss an easy black. Up stepped Davis, who had been reduced to the role of spectator, to take the frame 69–37 with a 45 break. His fans, who might have thought another of the famous Davis charges was beginning, were to be silenced almost immediately. Playing blistering snooker, Hendry rattled in a 58 break to win the seventh frame, 94–0, and lead the afternoon session 6–1. The unbeatable Davis had failed to score a single point in three of the frames.

In the press-room, the journalists, who have seen almost everything on the circuit, were as stunned as the millions of viewers all over the country. Joe Lancaster, the gravel-voiced North of England free-lance, summed it up: 'I do not believe what I am seeing. The kid is on fire.' Back in their hotel, there was no advice from the normally loquacious Ian Doyle. 'I just said to Stephen: "keep up the good work. You've been absolutely brilliant. Steve Davis is a goner."'

The semi-final resumed just after 7.15, and Hendry immediately re-established his authority. He conjured a 94 clearance to win 132–4 and forge even further ahead, 7–1. The ninth was his, 72–21, with a break of 54. It was just one frame away from a spectacular victory.

Davis, battered and bruised, picked himself off the floor with a brief but hopeless flurry. He took the tenth and eleventh frames 75–14 and 88–0 to trail 8–3. But, inevitably, it was to be Hendry's hour. He wrapped it up in the twelfth, 63–31, to roll the curtain down on Davis's four-year-long one-man show.

As the crowd roared, and the flash-bulbs exploded, the world's number one was gracious, and humorous in the midst of his shattering defeat. 'I know what went wrong,' he quipped to a television interviewer. 'I spent too much time sitting down, drinking water.' Then he added: 'I have no complaints. Quite simply Stephen was absolutely superb. Like the outstanding professional he is, he kept me down, and never really gave me a chance.'

Hendry breezed into the press-room, amazingly calm in the circumstances. 'It's a tremendous boost, especially getting the better of Steve over 17 frames, but to be honest I didn't think I would win so convincingly. It was like a jigsaw when everything seemed to fit into place.

'After leading 6–1, I knew deep down I couldn't be beaten. It was a case of sustaining the pressure, and not allowing Steve to sneak in the back door.'

He added: 'I know I can go the distance with anyone.' And he might have been forgiven for thinking that that anyone included Doug Mountjoy. The title, and the £80,000 first prize, seemed to be in the bag.

The bookies responded to his success by making him 4–1 on to lift the third major championship of his career. But it had also been an amazing tournament for the rejuvenated Mountjoy, a 46-year-old former coal miner, ranked number 24 in the world. Playing the best snooker of his life under the watchful eye of coaching guru Frank Callan, the man who has done so much to help Steve Davis, Mountjoy excelled himself *en route* to the final. But although he defeated former World Champion Terry Griffiths 9–5 in the other semi-final, no one was really watching. All eyes were on Hendry.

93

Mountjoy, however, was hungry. The past years had starved him of success. In 1987, he won just £27,516, peanuts by modern-day snooker standards. His previous highest earnings in one season totalled a little more than £48,000.

By contrast, in the 1987–88 season, Hendry lifted £283,114 in prize money, bettered only by Davis with £495,611.

Mountjoy clearly had a massive job to do with those powerful hands of his. But he warned Stephen: 'I've got a bit of experience. Who knows what might happen.'

Neither he, nor anyone else in the Guild Hall, would have predicted what did, in fact, happen in a final that began on Saturday, November 25, and was to stretch over 31 frames until the following night.

Hendry was on a high. What a week it had been. Even his favourite football team, Hearts, had dumped the Yugoslavs Mostar in a UEFA Cup tie at Tynecastle. But the glories of the week were soon dimmed. He was in trouble.

Mountjoy, playing with surgical precision, won the opening frame 75–26, and although Hendry levelled matters with a 103 break in the second, it was already clear that he had a fight on his hands. He notched up another 113 break in the fifth, but Mountjoy took the opening afternoon session 5–2.

Alarm bells were ringing faintly, but it was not yet time for anyone in the Hendry camp to press the panic button. Stephen's game had been strangely subdued. Between shots, he rested his head on his knees, occasionally rolling his eyes upwards to the roof. His mind seemed anywhere but the Guild Hall.

After the break, though, he began to click. This time, Doug was forced to sit back and admire the view, with Hendry rattling off the next four games, 65–62, 96–13, 89–14 and 72–37 to haul himself back to 6–6. His opponent responded with a workmanlike 48 break in the 13th, to edge back into the lead.

Hendry had saved the best for last. In the final frame of the day, he rifled in a break of 129 to level at 7–7, and set himself up for the £8,000 prize for the highest break of the tournament. The bookies weren't worried. They continued to make him 4–1 on with Mountjoy 3–1 against. But it was to be Black Sunday for Stephen.

The excuses for the stuttering Saturday were obvious, and freely given. Naturally Stephen had suffered a reaction to that amazing Davis triumph. Now he had that out of his system, just watch The Kid go. Everyone thought so. Everyone but a middle-aged Welshman with the battered look of a prize-fighter.

The afternoon of torture began quietly enough, with the 15th and 16th frames falling to Mountjoy, slow to watch compared to Hendry, but enormously effective. He took them 76–49 and 71–41, and still everyone waited patiently for Hendry to move into top gear.

What followed was astonishing. Mountjoy did to Hendry what Hendry had done to Davis – crushed him. With Stephen trapped forlornly in the glare of the television arc lights, Doug surged into a commanding 11–7 lead, winning the next frames 125–0 and 73–0.

The pain piled on. The next four frames went to the Welshman 71–21, 131–0 (giving him the £8,000 bonus for the highest TV break), 106–0 and 129–0. Between the 17th and the 22nd frames Hendry scored just 22 points. Mountjoy was 15–7 up, just one frame away from victory. His 131, 106 and 124 breaks equalled Steve Davis's world record of three successive centuries.

Hendry was shattered, but he was not about to

mark the end of his championship run by surrendering to a slaughter. He dug deep into the reserves, so depleted by the wins over Thorburn and Davis, and took the 23rd frame with a brave 96 break. Then he dragged his way back into the match by lifting the next four, 66–54, 73–5, 80–21, and 56–43.

It was 15–12, and what would have been the greatest comeback in big-time snooker was a possibility. No one had won a match eight frames down with nine to play.

But Hendry's revival came just too late. As thousands of eyes peered in from the darkness of the Guild Hall, his dream turned to dust. Mountjoy took the 28th frame 67–11 to win the final 16–12. Cheered on by his wife Yvonne, his family, and an army of Welsh fans, he broke down and wept. He had played the game of his life.

Stephen's sad eyes spoke volumes. Life had become very difficult all of a sudden. But he was philosophical enough in the moments of trauma. 'If I was to lose to anyone, I'm happy it was against Doug. During the afternoon session he played the best anyone has ever played against me.'

He added: 'Subconsciously, I probably felt that Doug could not beat me over 31 frames, so that was another invaluable lesson. Defeats like that put steel in your body.'

It should have been the greatest night of Stephen Hendry's meteoric career. The most glittering prize so far had been within his grasp. His greatest triumph, the demolition of Steve Davis, was still swirling around in his head. That was just the trouble.

He stood, utterly dejected, in Preston's Guild Hall and watched Doug Mountjoy, with tears in his eyes, holding aloft the trophy Hendry had been sure was his for the taking. Mountjoy, a reminder of older,

during the match. To set the record straight, what I actually said was that the game was so scrappy, the spectators must have found it boring. Unfortunately I was quoted wrongly, but that can happen.'

Misquoted or not, Stephen came in for some criticism, and he went on to bungle his bid to beat John Parrott in the semi-final, missing the chance for a final against Steve Davis, who had defeated Jimmy White, 9–5.

Against Parrott, Hendry trailed 3–0, then 5–3, before he found his touch to edge ahead 6–5. But he lost the twelfth, and after the interval could do nothing right as Parrott seized three in a row to win 9–6. Davis then overpowered Parrott 9–5 in the final.

For Hendry, there was a losing semi-finalist cheque for £20,000, but that was small consolation. Said Hendry: 'It was a big disappointment. I arrived in Brentwood with high expectations after reaching the final of the Tennents UK at Preston. Even though I lost to Doug Mountjoy, I felt I was playing well. But John played superbly, and I just didn't play as well as I can.'

Even so, Stephen was determined that 1989 was going to be his year. As he packed his bags for the first championship of the year, the Mercantile Credit Classic at the Norbreck Castle Hotel in Blackpool, he had every reason to feel optimistic.

With the tournament at the fourth round stage, he knew that Steve Davis was already out of the way, stunned by Welshman Tony Chappell in the previous round. Hendry's opponent was the cunning and vastly experienced Ray Reardon. Stephen won 5–4, despite Reardon displaying the kind of form that had made him a legend. 'I couldn't believe how well Reardon played that night. His safety play was impeccable, it was as if he had the white ball on a string.

'The break I made in the deciding frame was one of the best I've ever had. At 30 points down I made 72 to take the match, and I tell you I was very relieved to come through.

'Afterwards, during a television interview with Dickie Davies, Ray remarked that it was good to see a young player like myself sustaining such pressure. You never really like matches as tight as that! They do nothing for the nervous system.'

Hendry's next match was against Welshman Steve Newbury, and feeling good after the Reardon victory, he cruised through 5–1. So he was into the last eight and facing a meeting with Cliff Thorburn. 'I always knew it was going to be tough, for at that stage in my career, I was finding it really hard against these kind of players.

'The reason was simple. My safety was not up to scratch, and I was not potting as well as I would have liked. This time my concern was well founded. Thorburn soon put me in serious trouble and led 4–2. I fought back to level at 4–4, but he tied the game up in the final frame, and I could not get a look in. I lost 5–4.'

It was a real disappointment. 'I had to fancy my chance of winning that title, with Davis and Jimmy White already out. It left John Parrott and myself seeded to meet in the final. Looking back, however, my confidence was not 100 per cent.'

In fact, the Mercantile tends to be a killer for the big names. Against the odds, Doug Mountjoy, the unexpected UK champion, surprised everyone again by winning the final; a 13–11 victory over another Welshman, Wayne Jones.

What is it about the Mercantile Classic which transforms the Golden Mile into Skid Row for the superstars? Hendry commented: 'One of the reasons could be that the players are a shade rusty after being on holiday over Christmas and New Year. But that of course applies to every player, so no one can really make excuses. But it's a graveyard, all right!'

Shortly after his 20th birthday on January 13, Hendry's quest moved on to the Wembley Arena, and the Benson and Hedges Masters. It was his first appearance in the invitation event for the top 16 in the world – and he left London as the youngest-ever winner.

'It's got to be one of the world's top venues, and the atmosphere was incredible. I didn't play well in the first match, although I beat Willie Thorne 5–2. In the first four or five frames, I was overawed by the venue: it's such an imposing arena. The London fans really love their snooker, and they let you know it.

'In the quarter-final, I beat Terry Griffiths 5–3, and again I didn't play all that well. Luckily, neither did Terry and I scraped through.'

The semi-final brought the match everyone wanted: Hendry v Davis. Hendry started as the underdog, and won an intriguing contest 6–3. 'I played really well, and matched him shot for shot in every department. I punished him when I got in, and put him under pressure from the first ball.

'Having already beaten Davis 9–3 in the semi-finals of the Tennents UK in 1988, I wanted to prove I could beat him again and again – not just once.'

Against Davis, Hendry scored a 119 break, which was to be the highest break in the championship, earning him an extra £6,000.

A crowd of 2,800 watched Hendry's final against John Parrott. The first frame fell to the Liverpudlian with a 93 break, but Hendry went in at the interval leading 5–2. 'I was on song,' said Hendry, but then he could only watch as Parrott dragged back to 5–4.

Hendry was not to be denied. He stretched his advantage to 7–4, and finally left London with a

cheque for £62,000. Said Ian Doyle: 'It's always special when a player beats Davis, as Stephen did so handsomely in the semi-finals.

'Stephen beating Davis gave me considerable satisfaction. Probably, up until Stephen beat him in the Tennents, Davis had never acknowledged him as anything other than a headless chicken. But he now gives him the respect he deserves. He knows that Stephen is the one player on the circuit who can beat him on a regular basis.'

Of the final against Parrott, Doyle said frankly: 'The quality of the snooker was sometimes scrappy, but I always felt Stephen would come through.'

The snooker bandwagon had to come off the rails some time, and the crash came next in 1989. It was the sport's biggest flop: the ill-fated ICI European Open staged in the opulent surroundings of Deauville Casino in northern France.

Steve Davis had decided to cut down on his work schedule, and opted out of the tournament. He was not a bad judge of a tournament as it unfolded.

Stephen and 63 other hopefuls were there, aiming for a first prize of £40,000. 'Unfortunately, the French people in that wealthy part of the country were not exactly into snooker. At some of the matches, the crowds totalled less than a dozen – and most of them were players and officials.

'It was a very strange, unsettling experience. Deauville was very nice, everything about it was beautiful, and the casino was out of this world. But it was not the place to stage a top snooker cham-pionship. It was like playing in a morgue.'

Hendry's opponent for a place in the last 16 was Irishman Paddy Browne. And although there was no one to cheer him home, Hendry won easily enough, 5–0. In the fifth round, however, he went down 5–3 to Mike Hallett.

'I was 4–0 down at the interval, came back to

4–3, missed an easy ball, and Mike was through to the quarter-finals. I would not make excuses. Deauville was a disaster, but the lack of atmosphere was the same for every player. That night I think Mike was a lot more motivated than I was. He seemed to want to win very badly, and that was the difference.'

John Parrott went on to deflate Hallett 5–4, and then overcame Terry Griffiths 9–8 in the final. 'One

After winning the Stormseal UK Championship in 1989 having defeated Steve Davis

103

thing is certain,' said Hendry, 'no leading snooker event will ever again be staged in Deauville. In the words of John McEnroe, it was "the pits", at least as far as snooker was concerned.'

Hendry's next assignment was the Anglican Windows British Open at Derby, defending the title he won in 1988. After destroying Englishman Craig Edwards 5–0, his next match was against the talented but unpredictable New Zealander, Dene O'Kane.

Hendry won 5–2, and said: 'Dene is another player who tends to raise his game against me. He is very dangerous, and invariably plays well in our matches. Since I've moved up the rankings, I find that many players raise their game against me. Some think they have nothing to lose, and it can make life difficult, but it's certainly never boring. I'm up there to be shot at.'

Dapper Tony Meo stood between Hendry and a place in the last eight as the tournament rolled towards the crucial final stages at the city's Assembly Rooms. It looked like murder for Meo. But the likeable Londoner produced one of the shocks of the year, winning 5–3.

'I played some silly shots early on, and it cost me the game. Tony played better than he had done for over a year, but I did have the chance to win. I was 3–1 down at the interval, and never really recovered. Again it was very disappointing. No player likes to lose a title he is defending, especially in the early stages.'

Meo went on to show that his hammer blow over Hendry was no fluke. In the quarter-final he defeated Peter Francisco, followed by a 9–8 semifinal triumph over Mike Hallett. In a dour final, he battled to a 13–6 success over Dean Reynolds.

Hendry was happy for Meo. 'It's amazing the confidence a player will get if he beats a big name.

Clearly, Tony was on a high after beating me. I left Derby knowing I had a lot of work in front of me. I hate losing.'

Bournemouth was the setting for the Fersina Windows World Cup, the game's top team event. Hendry was accompanied to the resort's Conference Centre by fellow Scots, Murdo Macleod and Jim Donnelly. 'Somehow, this is a tournament I have never played well in, and this year was no exception. Everyone seems to give Scotland no chance, and it's a tournament which continues to elude us. While I always try my best in the World Cup, I prefer individual matches. The two-frame set-up is a killer, as you never get a chance to settle into any rhythm. A lot depends on the mood you're in. I didn't perform, and Wales beat Scotland 5–3.

'But as the game gets stronger in Scotland, our chances of winning the World Cup will improve. It's not an impossibility, and it would certainly give me a great buzz if we were to win. It's not about money. England beat the Rest of the World 9–8 to win the £43,200 first prize. What it boils down to is pride in your country, and I'm as patriotic as most Scots.'

The Benson and Hedges Irish Masters was to provide one of the highlights of 1989, and it ended with Irish eyes smiling. The venue was a horse sales ring in Goffs, County Kildare. 'It's a championship which will always be very special to me,' said Hendry. 'The countryside is marvellous, the people are fantastic, and the atmosphere at the tournament is electric.

'In my opening game in the quarter-final, I beat Terry Griffiths 5–2. That set up a semi-final with Steve Davis, and I got the better of him 6–4, which meant I had beaten him three times in succession. In fact, it was my fourth victory over Steve in one season. I don't think any other player has achieved that.

105

Resting prior to the final of the Irish Benson and Hedges, 1989

'My prospects didn't look too bright when I found myself trailing 3–1. But I came through, and also made the highest break of the championship, a 136, which earned me a £3,000 bonus.'

The real drama, however, was going on in the bottom half of the draw, where a guy called Alex Higgins was setting Goffs alight. He beat Cliff Thorburn 5–4, Neal Foulds 5–2, and John Parrott 6–4, then set his sights on Hendry in the sort of final that dreams are made of.

Said Hendry: 'I knew it would be a great final. I also wanted to do the double after my success in the Benson and Hedges final in London. But I was not prepared for what was to happen.'

With the Irish fans willing Higgins on during every shot, Hendry lost 9–8. 'It was a game I should never have lost. I got careless. I was 4–0 up and started to go for silly shots. The crowd were behind Higgins all the way. I would make a century break, and there would be a polite ripple of applause. Then Higgins would hit a few balls, and they went wild.

'I suppose it put me, unconsciously, under a lot of pressure. It was the first time in my career that I'd experienced such bias against me. But good luck to Alex. He showed flashes of his old genius, and judging by the cheers he received at the end, he was a very popular champion. But, as I said, I threw it away. I should have been shot.

'When I was in front 4–0, I relaxed my grip, and Higgins went in after the break 5–2 behind. Then he won the next four frames to go ahead 6–5. The Irish loved it; they were shouting their heads off. I was the bad guy and I knew it. In fact, it was more like a bull ring, than a horse sales ring. And with the Higgins supporters hanging from the rafters, I knew who the bull was supposed to be.

'Despite the uproar, I got my act together in the twelfth frame with a 109 break, to a brief ripple of appreciation, and took the next two to leave me just one frame away from the title, and a famous Benson and Hedges double. At that stage, 8–6 ahead, I thought I was home and dry.

'But Higgins showed what a fighter he can be, winning the last three frames with breaks of 54, 33 and 62 to win 9–8. I drove out of Goffs with just under £17,000, while Higgins was a national hero again. I let him off the hook, and I was angry about it.'

Hendry rates Goffs, along with Wembley, as the best snooker venue in the world.

The Irish loss had to be put to the back of his mind as the big month rolled up again: April, and the Embassy World Championship.

'I had practised like hell for this one. I wanted to do well for myself, my family, for Ian Doyle. I wanted so badly to bring the title back to Scotland. My preparations were perfect. Six hours locked away at Spencers snooker club in Stirling, potting ball after ball, day after day, so that I would be in tip-top shape.

'We – myself, Ian and the CueMasters driver John Carroll – don't stay at the Grosvenor Hotel in Sheffield, which is used by many other players, officials and the press. Instead, we prefer to stay at the St George Hotel which is off the beaten track, but very comfortable and well run.

'The first round of the Embassy is often dangerous ground for the top seeds. I remember Steve Davis was once hammered 10–1 by Tony Knowles in his opening match. I almost came a cropper too, against England's Gary Wilkinson. I knew it would be tough, because when I played him before I just came through in the final frame. And it happened again as I won 10–9. But everyone seems to struggle in that first round; you're under so much pressure.'

109

His reputation intact, but only just, Hendry returned to his hotel a much relieved young man. Next in his firing line was Willie Thorne, and Hendry discovered that top-level snooker is not just about potting balls. 'Willie is a master at trying to bring you down mentally before a match. He jokes, he laughs and he does his best to wind you up.

'I was on one practice table, when he came in. He had a suit on, took his cue out of his case, played for two or three minutes with his jacket on; took his jacket off, played for two or three minutes; put his cue in his case, and said to me as he walked out: "I don't need to bother, the white's on a string."'

'I remember I was wearing a shirt which had a trophy design on it, and he remarked: "That's the only way you'll get a trophy here." That's Willie. He loves a wind-up, and it gives me a laugh as well.'

'I might say to Willie: "How are you playing?" and he'll reply quick as a flash: "Three 147s, two centuries, and a couple of 90s. I'm playing like a donkey."'

But in the second round, Hendry had the last laugh as he despatched the wise-cracking Thorne 13–4 to reach the quarter-final. There he defeated his old adversary Terry Griffiths, one of the giants of the Crucible.

'It was not an easy draw. Terry is one of the toughest players around, especially when he's competing in the World Championship. It's a tournament that brings out the best in him. At the interval we were tied 4–4 and I thought he was playing well. But in the second session I played out of my skin, played tremendous snooker, and made a 141 into the bargain. Terry only took one more frame, and I left the arena very happy, winning 13–5.'

Now came a big moment in Hendry's life: the semi-final against defending Champion Steve Davis. 'It was my first Embassy semi-final, and I felt confident. It was also the first time I had played in a one-table situation at the Crucible. All other matches prior to the semis are contested on two tables, split by a giant screen. It's a totally different feeling. I felt quite daunted when I walked through the curtains and down the steps for the most important match of my life.

Stephen with cricketer Bob Willis after his Continental Airlines Masters win, 1989

Stephen's Dubai Classic win, 1989

'I couldn't get into it at all,' confessed Hendry, who found himself 10–2 down, and staring humiliation in the face. 'Davis's safety play was immaculate, as it always is. I still think that's what won him the World Championship. He was potting well, but not nearly as well as he used to. If I could have matched him in the safety department, I would have had a chance. Unfortunately, I just couldn't.'

The second session turned out to be one of the finest ever witnessed at the Crucible. Instead of rolling over, Hendry showed his class and his courage, as he set about Davis with every shot in his book.

In the next ten-frame session Hendry had Davis reeling. With a little good fortune, he might have won all ten. Instead he won seven, and returned to the hotel, trailing 13–9. 'I played some of the best snooker I've ever played. I lost a couple of frames through a bit of bad running, and miscued when I needed just two more reds, which allowed Steve to pinch the frame.

112

'I felt pretty sick to be four frames behind. Back at the hotel, I felt I was out of the Championship, that that was that. Next day, although I had a chance in the first frame, I didn't really feel the same. Davis, on the other hand, was in sight of the finishing post, and he won all three frames to take the semi-final 16–9.

'After that match, I felt wiped out. It was yet another lesson that no one can afford to let Davis get off to a flier. The same thing happened in the final, and he beat John Parrott 16–3. It was a sad end to the Championship for CueMasters, and I only had to look at Ian Doyle's face to see how desperately disappointed he was. Two players in the last four, and both of us failed.'

After his semi-final defeat by Steve Davis in the 1989 World Championship

113

However, there were still two events up for grabs – the Continental Airlines London Masters at the Café Royal and the Matchroom League which is staged nationwide.

Says Hendry – 'I had mixed fortunes in both competitions. In the Matchroom League I had to settle for second best to Steve Davis. That's life!'

But the next setting – London's Café Royal – could not have been more different. It's dinner jackets, big cigars, glasses of brandy, and a well-heeled audience.

'I beat Terry Griffiths 4–0 in the first round, and Steve Davis 4–1 in the semi-finals, which was very nice. And despite suffering from a virus, I managed to defeat John Parrott 4–2 in the final.' That earned Hendry £25,000. For him, at least, the streets of London seemed to be paved with gold.

Mum and Dad

But with all the talent, all the common sense in the world, Stephen still faces the danger and pitfalls that bedevil all top sports stars.

And Irene Hendry is only too aware of them.

'Now that Stephen is a professional and doing very well, a number of things worry me. One is money . . . and that power you think you've got because of it. The sad thing is that money seems to corrupt. When I look round at people in the snooker world who have a lot of money, there are only a few I can look at and think, well, they've stayed what I would term a "normal" person.

'What concerns me is that the money, the power and the fame tends to make some people in snooker think they are above the rules and laws which everyone else has got to abide by. They are allowed to lead a kind of life and do things which ordinary people frown on.

'I am not saying ordinary people never break the rules, never commit adultery, never get up to mischief. What is wrong is that some people in snooker think they can do whatever they want. That in my

115

Opposite:
Pondering the
next move at the
1986 World
Championship in
Sheffield

mind is very wrong, and I would hate to see Stephen falling into the same trap.

'The world Stephen is involved in is not the real world. There are the guys who take drugs, the guys who drink far too much, the guys who have different women every night. I don't want that life for my son.

'In a way Stephen was protected from the outside world because all he wanted to do was play snooker. He didn't want to know about discos or anything like that. When he got home from school he picked up his cue, raced for the bus, and went to his local snooker club. He stayed there until his dad picked him up at night.'

The young Stephen hardly even had time to make friends – and now it's even more difficult. 'He had one friend at that time,' Irene remembered, 'Roddie, who was nice lad. When we go over to Dalgety Bay now, Stephen will say: "I wonder what Roddie's doin'". But he won't go up to see him because he's frightened Roddie will think he's posing. I say "Let's go up and just knock on the door. He may not even live there now." But Stephen just says "no, no". I suppose Stephen is embarrassed at times at how famous he is.'

But the protection of the family is not always possible now. And Irene Hendry realises that Stephen will make his own mistakes. 'Will he handle the whole money thing? That's the big question. He has got to make his own mistakes, otherwise he will never grow up into a mature adult. The only way he can learn is by going through it. One thing is for sure; when he does make a mistake, it will be very much in the public eye.'

'Women? Stephen hasn't shown, so far, that he is interested in wild flings. He'll laugh and joke about it, and he sees other people do it. But he's more interested in a steady relationship.

116

The fruits of success. Taking delivery of his first Mercedes in 1987

'Let's face it, it's inevitable that women will chase him. He's young, good-looking, a "personality", who makes a lot of money from the game. And everyone knows there are snooker groupies on the circuit. There will always be women who wouldn't mind having an affair with Stephen. I worry, naturally, but I know Stephen is learning to handle these situations himself.'

A far more serious situation is the world of drugs. 'Stephen is terrified by drugs. I would hate to see him fall under the influence of some players — people he worships, people he idolises — who use drugs. That is a concern — for Stephen to show he is one of the boys.

'The impression he has always given me, though, is that he knows drugs are stupid, and that there is enough in life without needing to get involved in drugs to get a kick.'

If there is one thing that brings out Irene's protective interest even more, it's the often luke-warm support for Stephen in, of all places, Scotland. 'The Scottish fans could get behind Stephen a lot more than they do at present. It will always be the same in this country. People never give the deserved credit to sports figures, actors, personalities, or whoever is in the limelight.

'The Scots love nothing better than putting down people like Stephen. Sometimes it makes my blood boil. Once the Scots put someone on a pedestal, they cannot wait to pull him down again.

'Stephen, apart from the win in the Regal Masters in 1989, has had some poor results in Scotland. Perhaps it's because he tries too hard in front of the home fans, but it saddens me when he plays players such as Alex Higgins in Scotland, and it's Higgins who invariably gets the bulk of the support. Surely to God the Scots should be behind Stephen. And now that he is World Champion he has given his Scots fans plenty to shout about.'

Gordon Hendry never had any doubts that his son Stephen would scale incredible heights in world snooker. 'He was born to play the game,' says Gordon, whose youthful looks, at 41, make many people think he is actually Stephen's older brother.

While Gordon never managed to shine at the game, he believed that snooker has always been in the Hendry blood. 'My dad played bit, and was fairly useful, hustling for a few bob here and there. He used to play with Bert Demarco, one of Scotland's best known characters. My dad's talent did not rub off on me. You only need to watch me play to see why! But it must have rubbed off on Stephen, and it's fair to say I was the proudest dad in the world when he raised aloft that Embassy trophy at Sheffield.'

Stephen with his parents

Gordon, now divorced from Stephen's mum Irene, lives with 26-year-old Gillian at their home in Musselburgh. He has always played an important role in Stephen's career, especially when he looked after Stephen on the circuit between the age of twelve and 17.

'I enjoyed it a lot. I would drive Stephen around

and generally look after him. These were important years when Stephen needed guidance. I would like to think I helped him in his career.'

But at the age of 17 it was decided that someone else should look after Stephen during his extensive travels, which have taken him to just about every corner of the globe, and that man was John Carroll.

Says Gordon, 'I suppose it was for the best. It was unfair on Stephen having his dad by his side all the time. That's not the way for a young man to grow up. Now I have seen Stephen mature into a fine young man. But he was brought up well, and has turned out exactly the way we would have wanted him to be.

'I don't think winning the World Championship will change him. He is not the kind of person to let fame and money go to his head. He was always a nice kid when he was young. Lively, like any other lad. He loved sport; badminton and football were among his favourites.'

Gordon believes that Stephen could be at the top for a long time, but warns: 'It's always harder to retain a world title than win it for the first time. Stephen, however, has loads of character, and I know he will be up to the challenge at the Crucible next year.'

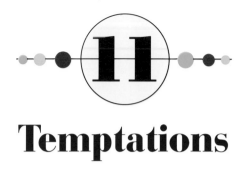

11

Temptations

Opposite: Mandy and Stephen

Not every man would consider women a hazard, but they can be when you are the world's number one snooker player.

'Stephen is hot property where some women are concerned,' is the verdict of Ian Doyle. 'He will be chased during his travels throughout the globe but I know he will handle the situation and not fall by the wayside as a few players have done in the past. Despite his young years, Stephen has become worldly wise. He doesn't get drunk and fall about. He's not into drugs. Stephen's only drug is snooker. It pumps through his veins. It's potting balls that gives him his biggest kick in life. As for women, he likes them as well as the next bloke. But he has a steady girlfriend just now, and is not the type to muck about with a relationship.'

Doyle is well aware of the pitfalls ahead of Stephen. And he has taken well planned steps to make sure that snooker's golden boy does not fall into the 'rat trap'.

For girls on the circuit are only too prepared to fall into Stephen's lap. They send him love letters, and the content can be naughty, to say the least. 'I laugh them off,' smiles Stephen.

Sometimes Doyle, however, does not laugh. Earlier this year, a newspaper – one of the tabloids – tried to set up Stephen in a potentially nasty situation, which was only averted by the security system which operates throughout the Doyle snooker network.

Ian takes up the story: 'It happened at a tournament in England. Two rather leggy ladies, dressed to kill, knocked on the door of Stephen's room late at night. But to their surprise it was our road manager, John Carroll, who answered the door just as the girls leapt forward, to be greeted by the pop of flash-bulbs from a waiting cameraman in the hotel corridor.

'It was clearly intended to get Stephen in a compromising situation. "Hot Snooker Ace in Late Night Love Triangle", or some rubbish like that.'

Doyle, however, cleverly messed up the proposed 'scoop'. 'When Stephen is playing at tournaments, we have a security measure where all telephone calls are either blocked or intercepted. That also applies to other players in the camp. We also switch their rooms so that unwelcome intruders, such as these two girls, don't know which room they are staying in.'

Says Ian: 'While we cannot protect ourselves from them all, we do our best.

'OK, there *are* outrageous womanisers on the circuit. Some players like to take advantage of whatever falls their way. But Stephen is not one of them.

'He's a snooker player, who wants to be at the top of the game for as long as he can.'

The love in Stephen Hendry's life is attractive 22-year-old blonde, Mandy.

Their six-year romance – which first blossomed in Wales back in 1984 – has not been without its share of heartache. At one stage Ian Doyle disapproved of their relationship, claiming that it was damaging Stephen's snooker career.

But in October, 1988, Mandy almost died in a car crash in Blackpool, which left her seriously ill. And there were only tears of joy in April 1990, when Mandy smothered Stephen in kisses, minutes after he captured the Embassy World Professional Snooker Championship.

'We are very close,' says Stephen, who at 21 is one of Britain's most eligible bachelors. 'Mandy and I share the same sense of humour. We have a lot in common, and she's great fun to be with.'

Stephen first met Mandy when he was playing in the Pontins tournament at Prestatyn in May 1984. He admits he liked her the second he saw her. 'She had lovely blonde hair and a smashing smile.' He was 15, and she was 16, but neither of them dreamed of the trouble which lay ahead.

Looking back to that first meeting Stephen recalls: 'Prestatyn is not exactly the most romantic setting on earth, but it did spark off something special for Mandy and me.'

In 1987, however, their romance had Doyle raging. Stephen had suffered two bad defeats in the Carling Champions tournament in Dublin, followed by the Langs Supreme Scottish Masters in Glasgow. Mandy had been there on both occasions as Stephen tumbled 5–3 to Dennis Taylor in Ireland, followed by a numbing 5–2 drubbing by Joe Johnson in front of a bitterly disappointed Glasgow public.

'It is true that I lost more games than I won when Mandy was with me,' admits Hendry. The Carling defeat was undoubtedly a blow, but if that was bad

then his beating by Johnson in the Langs Supreme was a nightmare. Hendry had come to Glasgow hoping to make amends for his 5–1 humiliation at the hands of Jimmy White in 1986.

Says Stephen: 'I played like a donkey against Jimmy and was determined to make amends.'

Once again, Hendry was a flop in front of a home crowd who must have been wondering why the snooker world was buzzing about the so-called Wonder Bairn. He led Johnson 2–0 and then fell to pieces as Joe ran home a comfortable winner.

'Both these defeats against Jimmy and Joe hurt like hell. People had paid good money to watch me and I let them down badly. It's difficult to say how much Mandy's presence affected my game. Certainly if she was at a tournament with me, I would try and spend as much time as possible with her but not to the detriment of my game. Maybe, indirectly, she did affect my concentration, although I was not aware of this at the time.'

Now the young couple – and Ian Doyle – have reached an understanding. Mandy stays away when Stephen is involved in competition. Indeed, at the 1990 Embassy World Championship, Mandy only arrived at about 8 pm on the Final Sunday, when the deciding session was already off and running.

Doyle is now a lot happier about their relationship. 'Stephen is a young man and there are always going to be problems along the road. Mandy's presence was a problem but that's fortunately been resolved. I have never had any objection to Stephen having girlfriends, as long as there were no interferences with his snooker career. Stephen's defeats in the Carling and the Langs were "down" moments in my life, because I did think at the time that Mandy was going to become a major headache.

'Certainly, Stephen and Mandy have been together for a long time and only the future will tell if they stay together. And while I hope they continue to be happy together, the main thing for me is that Stephen maximises what is a God-given talent.'

Certainly, when Stephen and Mandy are with each other, there is no hiding their mutual affection. Yet their romance was almost destroyed by the car accident in Blackpool, when a car in which Mandy was travelling hit a lamp-post. Recalls Mandy: 'I suffered a bruised brain, a broken pelvis, had 30 stitches inserted in a head wound, and spent four weeks in hospital. I'm still recuperating, for my balance is still a bit wonky. After the accident there were so many things I had to learn again, like brushing my hair. Nothing was simple then, but now, thankfully, I'm well on the road to recovery.

Mandy and Stephen with World Championship trophy, April 1990

127

'One thing that really upsets me, though, is that I can no longer show-jump, a sport I have always loved.'

Mandy admits that at the time of the accident she did not realise she was badly hurt. 'My life went past in a daze. Indeed, I spent a lot of time laughing at absolutely nothing in particular. Everything seemed so amusing. But it was a bad time for my family. Mum and Dad went through hell.'

'I'm just happy that Mandy is better,' says Hendry.

Mandy admits she is very fond of this amazing young snooker star whose earnings could top a staggering £2 million during his reign as World Champion.

'When we first met, Stephen was really shy, not arrogant like some people may have thought. Now he has a lot more confidence coupled with a great sense of humour. He makes me laugh a lot. He makes me happy.'

Mandy also has an astonishing admission to make. 'I hate snooker; it bores me. The only time I can be bothered to watch is when Stephen is playing. He is exciting, unlike some of the other players in the circuit who send me to sleep.'

Mandy also admits frankly that her earlier presence at tournaments in which Stephen was competing, *did* have an effect on his game. 'Maybe it was one distraction too many. Now I'm happy to stay away and catch the results on television or in the newspapers.'

Mandy is quick, meanwhile, to take a swipe at the rumour mongers who claim she is not in love with Stephen – but with his money. 'That's cruel and it's nonsense. When I first met Stephen he was a promising 15-year-old amateur who I liked very much. Outside Scotland he was not yet famous, or anything like that.'

Mandy openly admits that she took the first positive step in their romance. 'At the Pontins tournament we exchanged telephone numbers and I called Stephen two weeks later. Six years on, we are closer than ever. Basically Stephen is great to be with. We don't do anything wildly exciting when we go out but we both enjoy dinner together, most of the time at a Chinese or an Italian restaurant.'

Doyle *v* Hearn
The Managers'
Views

You have got to hand it to Matchroom entrepreneur Barry Hearn. The man has style. Instead of being upset by the downfall of Steve Davis, followed by Jimmy White in the 1990 Embassy World Championship, Hearn refused point blank to adopt a crestfallen attitude. The cutting down of Davis by White in the semi-final must have been a crushing blow, especially since Davis was within striking distance of a seventh world crown, which would have beaten Ray Reardon's modern-day record of six.

But even when he is beaten, Hearn never looks like a loser. He is all smiles; a man whose charisma, hard graft and love of life has lifted him to the top of the game. Hearn is also downright cheeky. Some would call him insolent.

I asked him how he felt now that Hendry had upstaged the great Davis as king of the snooker jungle.

Hearn's reply was instant. 'To my mind Stephen Hendry is not the best player in the world, although he is currently World Champion. It is not an essential requirement for a World Champion to be the best player in the world. Hendry has matured into a very fine player, three or four years quicker than most people would have thought possible – including myself. Hendry has knocked on the door of greatness. He has rung the doorbell, and next season will see if anyone is going to answer the door.'

Hearn firmly believes that Hendry has provided Davis with the spur he needs to rise from the ashes. 'Although Hendry might not realise it, he has added great motivation to Davis's life, and for that I would like to thank him. He has done one of two things. He will retire Davis or inspire Davis. It's my opinion that he will inspire him.'

Hearn went on frankly: 'What Davis experienced after the World Championship was a period of hurt for a while. But then I knew he would prepare himself for the challenge ahead.

'I am not trying to take away anything from Stephen Hendry. He played superbly and has shown what a great player he is. But then again, I am confident that Davis will respond to the challenge he has been handed.

'It's good for the game. Anything that can generate more excitement into the sport can only be good news.'

Hearn knows more about the psychology of sport than most people. That knowledge comes with looking after World Champions like Davis.

He says: 'It's interesting to compare Davis as a young player and Hendry as a young player. When Davis arrived on the scene, people claimed he lacked personality, that he came across as arrogant. The same has been said of Hendry. Such criticisms mean nothing, and are said by people who know nothing about sportsmen.

'Hendry's personality is now shining through, and that comes with confidence. He will need it next year for it's my firm belief that Davis is going to be a much harder player to beat. Of course, no one knows for sure who is going to come out on top between Davis and Hendry. And that's the great thing about the sport. There is always uncertainty and that's what makes people buy tickets.

'In this year's World Championship it was always going to be a dogfight between Davis and Hendry. I was convinced that Steve would win, but equally sure that Stephen would take the title once Jimmy had beaten Steve. And that's taking nothing away from Jimmy White. Next year, however, I'm going for Davis to recapture his old form and win the World Championship for the seventh time.

'There are exciting times ahead in the game. Two players, Hendry and Davis, will be especially motivated. Their rivalry will become even more intense over the next two or three seasons. I see it all head to head between the two players. I honestly do not see anyone else coming through to challenge them.

'It's nice in life to see people do well, and despite the banter we have, Ian Doyle comes into that category. In the past I have criticised Doyle for inexperience. But I have always said he is a grafter and that's a quality I admire in anyone. I know we will continue to work well together.

'You view the world differently when you have a World Champion. For a start you have more fun. In my early days in snooker I was as serious as anyone but that changed when Davis won his first world title, beating Cliff Thorburn in 1983.'

On Hendry's future, Hearn says: 'Stephen is now among snooker's elite, and it's a question of him living with that reputation. He has got more things to prove and will be striving for even more consistency.

'We live in a tabloid society and people are looking for someone new all the time. Results are the only thing that don't lie.'

Launching Stephen's new 'spike' haircut in 1987

Where does Steve Davis go from here? 'Regrettably, the only way he can go is down,' is the frank assessment of Ian Doyle.

The CueMasters supremo predicts tough times ahead for Barry Hearn's snooker legend, saying: 'It's going to get more and more difficult for Steve, especially now that Stephen is World Champion and world number one.

'I'm certain that Davis has the ability to remain in the top three for the next three or four years and that would be acceptable for just about every leading professional in snooker. But I am not too sure if Davis will be able to cope with that mentally. He is a magnificent player who ruled snooker for a decade. Everything he wants in snooker is to be the best. And now the fact that he is no longer the best could cause him all sorts of anguish. It will be very interesting to see how he reacts to the situation. Personally, I think his glory days are over. That happens in every sport for no one can go on forever, much as they would like to.'

Doyle has scrutinised Davis – on and off the table – closer than most people. And he doesn't miss a thing. Says Doyle: 'I watch the way he eats; the way he drinks a pint. There are a lot of things I know about Davis that he is probably unaware of. For example, he gets worried about who may be driving with him. He does not like excessive speed. He enjoys eating Marks and Spencer sandwiches on a regular basis.

'Davis is a creature of habit. That is not a criticism. Of course, his biggest habit has been winning. It hurt him badly when he lost the world finals of 1985 and 1986 to Dennis Taylor and Joe Johnson. Now I believe Davis has a mountain to climb which he may find insurmountable.'

Doyle is only too aware that some people will point out that Stephen won the world title, but did it without having to meet Davis in the final. Such talk does not annoy him. He merely laughs and says: 'First and foremost you must bear in mind that

Davis was not good enough to get into the final. To be honest, Davis was fortunate because he would have been hammered, and that may well have added even further to his mental anguish.

'In his semi-final against Jimmy he made a lot of elementary mistakes. Jimmy defeated Steve, because for once in his life he did not allow himself to be pulled into the Davis trap. He, and not Davis, played the balls. He refused to be intimidated and deserved to win.

'As for Davis, it's a simple fact that he has not been scoring as heavily as he used to. He is finding it more and more difficult to finish off a frame in one visit. In saying that, I'm not taking anything away from Jimmy. To beat Davis at the Crucible was a fabulous achievement. Equally, if Steve had faced Stephen in the final, he would have been wiped off the table – murdered.'

Doyle believes that the Davis Fear Factor played a major role in his dominance of snooker over the years.

'I have seen Davis win matches he had no right to win. He won because of the pure fear he inflicted on his opponents who believed, before a ball was struck, that they could not beat him.

'Hendry is now doing the same to his opponents. There are now a number of players in the game who know they cannot beat Hendry. They know he is that good. And that includes some guys in the top ten who, if they live to be 100, will be lucky to defeat Stephen in one in 50 matches.'

Hendry is the most marketable snooker player in the world. 'He's up there with the *big* names in British sport, with guys such as Nigel Mansell and Nick Faldo,' says Doyle.

But while Doyle knows that Hendry is already worth a king's ransom he insists: 'Stephen Hendry's contract is not for sale, unless someone arrives at my door with the Crown Jewels. Stephen is priceless to me. I could not, would not put a figure on his contract because that is not an option. In any case, money has never been a major factor for me in the snooker business. I am not into the buying and selling of human flesh. I do my best for my players to the best of my ability. My one ambition in CueMasters is to see that everyone I represent maximises his ability both professionally and financially.'

Doyle is a man who will never be bullied by any of his players. 'If anyone is unhappy with what I'm doing for them, they are free to leave. I've had players come into my office in Stirling asking for, maybe, more money. My reply has always been the same. I walk through the office, dig out their contracts, their individual company books and hand them over. So far, no one has left in a situation like that. They all know they have an option, that they can walk out the door and never come back. But I know they will not get better snooker management anywhere else.

'Snooker is not a business for me, although the rewards are high. It's a hobby. Winning is life and death to me. Never at any time of my life have I believed that finishing second in anything is an achievement. No one remembers the runners-up.'

Doyle beams with pride, and rightly so, when he talks about what Hendry has achieved in such a short space of time. 'I have never made any claims that Stephen would become the youngest World Champion. But I knew in my heart that one day he would capture the title. Stephen did say in 1986 that he would win the World Championship in five years, and he has done that in style. That was quite a bold statement at the time, and I know there were people who sneered. But we believed that with the right amount of hard work and application, he would make that dream come true.

'I have no doubts that Stephen could become the greatest player to grace the game as long as he remembers the discipline, and the rules and regulations surrounding his public life. Today, alongside Davis, he is the most professional player in the world. In terms of pure professionalism there are probably no more than ten players who can go to corporate evenings, company exhibitions and that sort of thing, and conduct themselves on a completely professional footing. Stephen is one of that elite group in snooker, and to achieve that at the age of 21 is marvellous.

'My whole philosophy has been based on Davis, the perfect professional on and off the table. It annoyed me when people branded him the Romford Robot. He is not a Robot. He plays the game to win. For me he is the Jack Nicklaus of snooker. He has always preached total professionalism and sadly there are players who are jealous of what he has achieved.'

Doyle has already said where he thinks Davis's career is heading.

But where does Ian Doyle go from here? 'It's probably fair to say that nothing in snooker will ever surpass my feelings for Stephen's victory in the World Championship. It's the biggest achievement of my life to see a youngster work and learn the way Stephen has done. To achieve what he has done as a youngster is straight out of the pages of Roy of the Rovers.'

If Hendry successfully defends his world title in Sheffield next year, manager Doyle is convinced it will be a much more enjoyable occasion.

'The pressure is off Stephen now that he is World Champion. To be honest, his triumph in Sheffield was a nerve-racking experience. If he does the business next year – and he must have an outstanding opportunity – there will be much less pressure on Stephen and everyone else in the camp.

'I've still goals in my life. I want to see Stephen win more titles than Davis; I want to see everyone in the CueMasters camp do as well as they can.'

Doyle will also continue to gun for Barry Hearn and the Matchroom team. And he laughed aloud when Hearn, immediately after the World Championship, declared 'war' between the two camps. Said Hearn: 'The English built Hadrian's Wall to keep out the Picts. We are going to build an even bigger wall to keep out CueMasters.'

Smiles Doyle: 'I cannot really believe that statement from Barry. Matchroom are also-rans. If I was Barry, I would raise the white flag and surrender.

After the 1988 British Open final which Stephen won from his CueMasters stablemate, Mike Hallett, 13–2. Ian Doyle holds the trophy

There are too many players in Matchroom who are no longer capable of delivering the goods. They are either not good enough, or too old. Davis is the flagship, but as I've said before I believe that even the mighty Steve is sinking, slowly but surely. Matchroom's biggest problem will be coping with Stephen Hendry.

'Steve got his MBE by the time he was thirty . . . . Stephen could go one higher with a Knighthood. Wouldn't that be something for Scotland?'

Outside snooker, Doyle could be heading down even more exciting avenues. 'I have been approached by racing drivers, motor cyclists and football players and maybe I will diversify a little bit. In snooker I can see CueMasters staging its own

A family gathering the day after the final. Stephen with his girlfriend Mandy. Stephen's mother, Irene, centre back, father Gordon on Stephen's right behind the World Championship trophy, and brother Keith, third left, together with aunts, uncles and grandparents

events, perhaps. Maybe we will look at forming our own television production company. But snooker is the game I love more than anything else, and at my age I don't want to change too much.'

While Hendry invariably grabs the lions share of the headlines, Doyle has every reason to feel pleased with the progress made by the other members of the CueMasters stable.

'Mike Hallett won the Hong Kong title; Darren Morgan lifted the Welsh title, and reached the last eight of the World Championship before going down to Stephen. Gary Wilkinson reached the semi-finals of three ranking tournaments and is definitely one to watch for the future.

'Nigel Bond is also making meteoric advances, and I reckon he is a far better player than James Wattana. Martin Clark came through a traumatic time after his involvement with the Krugar Organisation. He is a player with great flair, and next season will make leaps and bounds.

'As for Joe Johnson, he has won one world title and appeared in a losing final. Joe has tons of ability. All he has to do is start believing in his unquestioned ability. Any man who can win a World Championship has got to be a great player, and I'm confident that Joe has titles left in him yet.'

Where Next?

Where does Stephen go from here?

Manager Doyle has no doubts when he says – 'The sky's the limit and I can see him dominating the game in the years to follow – just like Steve Davis did.

'For someone who is still only 21, what Stephen has already achieved in the game is phenomenal. In the season 1989–90 he appeared in ten major finals, winning eight. That brings his total title tally to 17, a feat that most players could only dream about.'

Doyle puts Hendry's rivalry with Davis in perspective when he points out: 'Davis was 23 before he lifted his first major title. How many more titles will Stephen have won by the time he is 23?'

The question that many people ask is: 'Will Hendry retain his hunger for the game now he is World Champion and world number one?'

Doyle is quick to reply: 'Stephen is as determined as ever. Snooker is in his blood, it's what drives him on in life and his goal is to win more titles than Davis.

'It's not an easy task, far from it. But Stephen has the ability and the tenacity required to become possibly the greatest ever player to grace a snooker table.

'He is the man everyone will be gunning for, but he has always revelled in challenge and I am totally confident he will handle everything that is thrown at him.

'Basically Stephen is a winner, he hates losing — just the same as I do — and has no intention of sitting back on his world throne. He wants to beat the hell out of everyone, whether it's Davis, White or any of his stablemates in the CueMasters camp.

'What I admire about Stephen is that he never boasts about his achievements. He prefers doing all his talking on the table — and he does that superbly. Personally I cannot wait for the new season. There are exciting times ahead but we are both aware there will be disappointments also.'

Will Hendry surpass Davis's achievements? Only time will tell . . .

Stephen Hendry
Principal Matches

1986	March	Canada Dry Scottish Pro Championship	beat	Matt Gibson	10–5
1987	March	Peoples Scottish Pro Champion	beat	Jim Donnelly	10–7
	July	Winfield Australian Masters	beat	Mike Hallett	371–326
	October	Rothmans Grand Prix	beat	Dennis Taylor	10–7
	December	Fosters World Doubles (M. Hallett)	beat	Taylor/Thorburn	12–8
1988	February	Britannia British Open	beat	Mike Hallett	13–2
	March	Swish Scottish Pro Championship	beat	Murdo Macleod	10–4
	May	New Zealand Masters	beat	Mike Hallett	6–1
1989	January	Benson & Hedges Masters	beat	John Parrott	9–6
	May	Continental Airlines London Masters	beat	John Parrott	4–2
	August	Asian Open	beat	James Wattana	9–6
	September	Regal Masters in Scotland	beat	Terry Griffiths	10–1
	November	Dubai Classic	beat	Doug Mountjoy	9–2
		Stormseal UK Championship	beat	Steve Davis	16–12
1990	February	Benson & Hedges Masters	beat	John Parrott	9–4
	April	Embassy World Championship	beat	Jimmy White	18–12
	May	Continental Airlines London Masters	beat	John Parrott	4–2

Losing Finals (runner up)

1986	December	World Doubles (M. Hallett)	12–3	Davis/Meo
1988	November	Tennents UK Open	16–12	Doug Mountjoy
1989	September	BCE International	9–4	Steve Davis
1990	March	European Open	10–6	John Parrott